THE OPERA
ACCORDING TO BARTALINI

Marilyn Mandler

THE OPERA

ACCORDING TO BARTALINI

A BOOK OF

DOGGEREL

LIBRETTI &

COMICAL

ILLUSTRATI

POMEGRANATE ARTBOOKS   *San Francisco*

Published by Pomegranate Artbooks
Box 6099, Rohnert Park, California 94927

Library of Congress Cataloging-in-Publication Data

Bartalini.
    The opera according to Bartalini : a book of doggerel libretti &
comical illustrati.
      p.   cm.
    ISBN 1-56640-994-2 (pbk.) : $19.95
    1. Opera—Humor.   I. Title.
ML65.B33   1994
782.1'0207—dc20   94-12809
                                            CIP
                                           MN

Designed by Bonnie Smetts Design

First Edition

Printed in Korea

ONTENTS

INTRODUCTION

"Oh, joy supreme," we hear her scream,
"Alfredo!" In he flies.
It won't be long. Soon she'll be strong.
All wrongs he'll rectify.

Oh, joy. Oh, glee. They'll leave Paree
Her health he'll soon restore.
She starts to cough. The trip is off.
She sinks unto the floor.

The death scene of *La Traviata* is thus interpreted by the skilled pen and sharp wit of Bartalini, who has applied his satirical insights to several operas in his rhymed rewrites of complete librettos. But Bartalini doesn't stop there: he fuels the hilarity with his charming and unforgettable watercolors of operatic drama, complete with scheming, licentious rakes and wild-eyed heroines armed with daggers. In entering the world of opera through Bartalini's interpretations, one is encouraged to guffaw loudly at the unlikely plots and dim-witted protagonists of those usually staid and proper musical extravaganzas.

Gualtiero Bartalini knows of what he mocks. Now retired, he was a concert artist, master of pantomime and producer of his own one-man show, "The Incomparable One-Man Theater: The Man of a Thousand Faces." His performance included opera arias, dance, poetry readings, monologues and impressions ("I could always imitate languages, and that ability to imitate is what started me on my career as a one-man theater"). He has performed all over the world.

Upon his retirement from show business, Bartalini purchased a San Francisco mansion on California Street, where he lived for forty years. He became the host of the city, entertaining friends and visiting opera stars and other celebrities on a nightly basis. Today, he continues to hold social court regularly from his apartment's living room and is one of San Francisco's favorite *bons vivants*.

Bartalini was born in Italy sometime around 1900 and has been singing opera arias since he was a child. His aunt Tina Graziani was an opera singer who created the title role in Charpentier's *Louise* at La Scala in Milan, and his mother's family in Italy hosted weekly music soirees visited by such notables as Puccini, Catalani and Forzano. Bartalini came to America with his family when he was four years old, and they settled in Sacramento. His mother taught him to sing, and he made his debut at the age of seven. He could speak five languages by the age of twenty-three. In the 1920s he moved to San Francisco.

It wasn't until he was in his eighties that Bartalini began to paint his very funny watercolors depicting scenes from operas. He first joined eighteen of these with his irreverent librettos in a self-published book, *Opera Psychotherapy*, in 1981.

It is Bartalini's intimate knowledge of the world of opera that allows him to respect it and poke fun at it at the same time. As he says, "I can still manage to squeeze out a tear, or even two, whenever a tubercular heroine starts to expire to the immortal strains of Verdi or Puccini," but, also, "One has to be truly a music depressive to take most [opera librettos] seriously. I'm afraid, to paraphrase Shakespeare, 'Time has withered and custom has staled their infinite variety.'"

Bartalini's words and pictures leave us anything but stale, and withered, perhaps, only as a result of laughing too hard.

La Bohème

This little gem is La Bohème
By Mürger and Puccini
About four hippies and two broads.
One's got TB; that's Mimi.

The male quartet labor and sweat
To live *la vie bohème*;
Living content, not paying rent,
And nonchalant ad nauseam.

Rodolfo, he writes poetry.
Marcello paints red seas.
Schaunard composes melodies.
Colline writes philosophy.

It's Christmas Eve, but they should grieve
For lack of food and heat.
Rodolfo burns immortal odes
To warm his seat and feet.

And here's Schaunard, the music bard,
With dough, food, and wine—the best.
'Tis said his music's fit to kill
Not soothe the savage breast.

Now all but one leave to have fun;
The poet stays behind.
He feels a sonnet coming on
Or maybe just a rhyme.

The girls are pert. They do fancy work;
That is, in their own way.
Mimi, she does embroideries;
Musetta, well, who is to say?

As Rudolph writes into the night,
He hears a gentle knock.
"Who could it be so late?" says he.
"It's almost twelve o'clock."

Timid with fright, without a light,
Mimi stands at the door.
He greets her graciously and thinks,
"Where have I seen that face before?"

She's quite afright, also uptight.
Her candle light blew out.
What can she do, this ingenue;
She's lost her whereabouts.

She gets a light all right, all right.
She thanks him and departs.
"Ah, woe is me," she's lost her key.
We're right back from the start.

She's out of breath. She coughs, bereft;
Collapses on a chair.
He sprinkles water on her face,
With overwhelming loving care.

"A spot of wine?" She first declines,
Then says, "Well, just a bit."
It's love all right. Love at first sight.
What else? Of course, that's it.

"Do calm your fears. Don't worry, dear.
No doubt it's on the floor."
He finds it; hides it in his smock,
While they proceed to search some more.

And as they search, grope, and re-search,
He reaches for her hand.
And then he goes from bad to verse.
Poetic license—understand?

"Your tiny hand, so cold, so bland,
Is frozen; but let's talk of me.
My field is lyric poetry;
My goddess is Calliope.

"A *bel esprit*, a bonhomie,
That's me. That's who I am.
Now tell me all about yourself,
I beg you. Oh, please don't scram."

"*Mi chiamano* Mimi," says she,
"But really Lucy is my name.
I knit and do embroidery.
My story's brief—always the same."

"Oh, lovely maid, do not evade
Though your story may be brief.
So join the group. Give up your job.
You can apply for state relief!"

It's Christmas Eve. She starts to leave.
He begs her to remain.
He gives her tea and sympathy
And other things humane.

It's clair de lune—a night to spoon.
His passion starts to burn.
He'll take her to Café Momus
And have fun on their return.

From down the yard, they call the bard,
"The friends—the bons vivants—await.
Don't be too long. Come right along,
And if you have one, bring your date."

So arm in arm, with loving charm,
They leave the attic niche.
They're in the hall. The curtain falls.
"*Amor, amor,*" they sing—off pitch.

ACT II – *The Latin Quarter*

Her artisans and charlatans
Foregather and cut loose,
Such gaity. Such camaraderie,
Especially *chez* Café Momus.

The musketeers assemble here;
That's what the four are called.
Now Mimi's added to partake
Of Latin Quarter bacchanal.

Soon on the set arrives Musette,
The part-time sweetheart of Marcel.
They've had another feud and spat,
But she's got stuff, so what the hell.

Musetta works. She does not shirk.
She also loves the baritone.
The work she does? Well, who are we
To criticize or cast a stone?

But here she comes with great aplomb
In Paris fashions à la mode.
With her old "patron," as they're called,
Which makes Marcello fume—explode.

She's mad as hell because Marcel
Pretends to see her not.
So just to catch his eyes and ears,
Her song of walking streets she starts.

When all signs fail, she starts to wail.
"A shoe," she screams, "pinches my toe."
The old roué starts on his way
To have it stretched, the dear old beau.

With bumps and grinds, the concubine
Wins back her love, her paramour.
It may not last because of spats,
But anyway, tonight for sure.

ACT III

It's early morn, before the dawn.
A tollgate is the scene.
A tavern lies behind the gate
And custom officers are seen,

Warming their seats, their hands, and feet
Around a brazier center stage.
Peasants arrive with hens and eggs,
And other products pasturage.

Mimi appears, coughing, in tears.
She begs a cop to fetch Marcel
Who's painting tavern signs for meals
And things to eat on walls, as well.

He sees Mimi, frail, fidgety.
She's had another awful spat.
And in a fit of jealousy,
Rodolfo went and left her flat.

It so appears Rudolph is here.
Marcello calls the *bon ami*.
Quick, Mimi hides behind a tree,
Where all can see her but not he.

At first the bard is rather hard;
Complains that Mimi is a flirt.
Marcel declares he's not sincere.
Then Rudy says that he's been hurt.

And then he adds she's failing fast;
Her coughing racks her slender frame.
And even if Mimi is fat,
The words are uttered just the same.

Poor Mimi hears, trembles with fear.
What can he mean? The words are dire.
She vacillates, then starts to cough,
Then in his arms again respires.

She starts a song that's rather long—
That is—only to say good-bye.
Then she decides she'll stick around
Till flowers bloom; then she must fly.

He says, "Okay. Have it your way.
At least on winter nights, we'll cling.
Then when one has to go, one goes,
Whether it's summer, fall, or spring."

ACT IV

It's now Act Four; the same decor,
As in the scene for Act One.
Rudolph is brooding for Mimi.
Marcel broods for that other bum.

Again some food changes the mood.
Two other roommates come with bags
Containing wine, herrings, and bread,
And, oh, so gay—those scalawags.

Like four gourmets they act and play,
Pretending water is champagne.
They dance quadrilles and minuets,
So fancy free, so addled brain.

The fun and sport is soon cut short.
Musetta bursts in, out of breath.
Mimi is climbing up the stairs,
Pallid and worn, of life bereft.

Mimi is led to Rudolph's bed.
She knows the way; been there before.
She's been abandoned by some guy
And yearns to see her love once more.

'Mid tears and grief, to bring relief,
The friends again take things to pawn:
Musetta's earrings and a coat;
Colline even rates a song.

Then as they go, pianissimo,
Mimi calls Rudolph to her bed.
"I feigned to sleep," we hear her say,
"To be alone with you instead."

Like homing doves (that rhymes with love)
He starts to think in metaphors.
"Your frozen hands, I'll warm with mine,"
And then he goes on with some more.

The friends return with drugs and stuff,
But cruel fate, alas, too late.
The end has come for Mimi dear.
She coughs and suffocates.

Tristan *und* Isolde

*T*ristan told the Cornish king he'd take care of everything.
He promised and he swore, in fact, that he'd bring Isolde back intact.
They are both aboard at last. Tristan goes before the mast.
Isolde thought, somewhat upset, "Is this English etiquette?
After all he pledged and said, is he playing hard to get?"
Whereupon Tristan appeared, saying, "Please excuse me, dear,
But I had to tell the crew the course to steer and pursue."
"Well, you know, Tristan," she said, very bold and spirited.

"Fact is since we cannot wed, why should we not both be dead?
Make a love pact suicide, die together—side by side.
Love like ours can never die," so she said, "why don't we try?"
"Gott," he said, taken aback, "true, we've reached a *cul de sac*.
That's indeed a strange idea," Tristan answered without cheer.
"Okay, Tristan," Isold' said, "that's decided, no more said."
So she called her faithful maid, who came quickly to her aid.

In Brangaene she confided, told her what she had decided.
"Mix some hemlock with some tea, that Hibernian recipe!"
"Okay," said the trusted maid, but for once she disobeyed.
No, Isolde must not die, so the order she defied.
Thus she mixed a recipe, Lipton's tea with LSD.
'Twas an Irish recipe, from some gremlins and banshees.
They're much smarter than is Cupid, and not nearly half as stupid.
"You drink first," said Belle Isold', handing him the chalice bold.

The eternal Eve once more, "You drink first, dear," that old bore.
Tristan drank at her command, then she snatched it from his hand.
Drained the chalice without dread, then awaited to be dead.
But the would-be deadly potion filled them both with strange emotion.
The brew was, matter of fact, a strong aphrodisiac.
Made *L'aprés Midi d'un Faun* look pathetic from then on.
They were no more seen at all, till they finally reached Cornwall.
King Mark was there to meet his bride, fossilized and Argus-eyed.

He had sent without delay the *Cordon de Sûreté*.
When knights of old went on Crusades, they protected wives and maids.
Scandalmongers used to say locksmiths worked both night and day.
Like Houdini did their best to free ladies in distress.
Anyway, old Mark was there, to take over and take care.
Afterwards the two were wed, Spring and Winter, people said.
But Isolde on the sly met Tristan. But by and by
Old King Mark at last got wise, so he sent Melot to spy.

13

ACT II – *The Garden of the King's Palace*

In the garden, fearless, bold, Tristan and Isolde stroll;
Heedless that they're being seen by Melot, vicious and mean.
An informer and courtier, Melot screens them everywhere.
He's been hired by old King Mark, whose bite is worse than his bark.
He is old, petulant, cranky, and won't stand for hanky-panky.
He is mad, sad, and forlorn, 'cause he feels but can't perform.
He can't rise to an occasion, so he's filled with grim frustration.
He has had an EKG—not as good as it might be.

And he also has to worry about strokes and coronaries.
Then the old gink pulls a stunt, says he's going on a hunt.
It's a ruse and an excuse, just to catch them on the loose.
He's informed by vile Melot, that the two are you-know-what.
So old Mark returns but fast, finds them kissing—he's aghast.
"I'm betrayed by my own kin, whom I've seen through thick and thin.
Bring her back intact, indeed, that fat-headed Ganymede."
Thereupon a fight ensues, for this moral turpitude.

Battle-axes, lances fly. Tristan gets the worst, poor guy.
Kurwenal, his good old friend, brings him home, hoping he'll mend.
Melot struck a mortal wound, with a poisoned sharp harpoon.
Tristan's lot is not so hot, much worse than was Lancelot's.
Lancelot grew hair and beard 'cause he flopped with Guinevere,
Went to pieces then and there, lived in caves in deep despair.
One could smell him miles away, so at least said good Elaine.
But, who cares 'bout Lancelot! Let's get back to Tristan's lot.

He's been hacked beyond repair; can't survive the wear and tear.
Meanwhile Mark has change of heart, so with Melot he departs.
He'll give up *la belle* Isold' to his nephew brave and bold.
It will be a big surprise, as with soldiers they arrive.
Big surprise, I'll say, and more, Kurnwenal thinks it means war.
Isold', too, is on her way; she's been warned. She's in dismay.
With enchantments, magic spells, Mark thinks Tristan will get well.
From the ramparts trumpets blare—she is coming—she is there!

Tristan rushes to her side, tears his bandages and flies.
And he gets there just in time to drop dead before her eyes.
She must die, too. There's no hope. It is in her horoscope.
Ere she dies, she clears her throat, sings her swan song, *Liebestodt.*
It's of love pure and inspired, so she sings and then expires.
Liebestodt, Ach, Liebestodt, get a load of *Liebestodt.*
Everyone dies. Two are left—Mark, Brangaene—sad and bereft.
King Mark kneels and prays in pain. The curtain falls— *auf Wiedersehen.*

SAMSON and DELILAH

The city of Gaza's the opening scene.
The Hebrews are threatened, defied, and demeaned.
They're affronted and menaced by the vile Philistines.
A fight to the finish is predicted, foreseen.

Even then they were struggling it out to obtain
The strip of the Gaza again and again.
Their one hope was Samson, the heavyweight swain,
Who developed his brawn but neglected his brain.

The Hebrews were beating their breasts at the Wall;
Their cries and laments filled the air like a squall!
They depended on Samson, who hated to brawl,
Saying, "Trust in the Lord. He'll settle it all!"

The Philistines feared the heavyweight jerk
With the strength of a bull (a most secretive quirk).
The Hebrews at last got mad, frantic, and irked
As the heavyweight champ flexed his muscles and smirked.

The Satrap of Gaza made the Jews sore as hell.
"God couldn't care less," said the hostile rebel.
In the chaos that followed, the battle to quell,
Samson slayed Abimelech, the snide infidel.

The Philistines gathered and worked out a scheme:
"*Cherchez la femme!*" said one of the team.
"Who else but Delilah, the harlot supreme?"
"Of course, let's get going!" cried the smart Philistines.

Delilah, the wanton, was ready to go.
When a man asked a favor, she'd never say no.
Yes, indeed, she knew Samson. In fact, time ago
She was jilted by him, just in case you don't know.

The Philistine meanies were bound and hell-bent
To discover the secret of Samson's great strength.
It was up to Delilah to brainwash the gent.
"This is grist to my mill," she said as they went.

By hook and by crook word reached Samson's ear;
He was told that Delilah still loved him most dear,
That she never forgot his muscles and hair.
The flattery did it; he'd rush to her lair.

Act II

As he entered the parlor he said, "Hello, toots!
They gave me the word at the athletes' kibbutz.
I jogged all the way, babe, sure did, bet your boots,
When I heard you were willing to again get cahoots."

Delilah said, "My heart opens when I hear your voice,"
And poor, dumb, stupid Samson lost all of his poise.
Standard equipment was straight Samson's choice,
So he did what he did, relaxed and rejoiced.

She said, "Tell me, my love, ere you slumber away,
Tell your Delilah, where does your strength lay?
Whisper it softly, a breath, a soufflé."
"In my hair," said the dope, in sleepy dismay.

She soothed him to sleep, held him close to her breast.
When he got exhausted, she laid him to rest.
Then she ran for her scissors, the sharpest, the best;
Cut off all his hair with a kiss and caress.

When Samson awoke from his deep dream of peace,
He started to curse, to scream, and to weep.
"Who done it," he said, "while I was asleep?"
"'Twas I," said Delilah, "you heavyweight creep!"

She then made a sign, a command like a queen;
Then in rushed the foes, the vile Philistines.
They grabbed poor weak Samson, who stumbled, careened;
Mocked, "Show us your muscles!" then vented their spleen.

From the prison of Gaza Samson was led
By a child, while vile insults were hurled at his head.
Delilah is there with her B.C. jet set,
Screaming insults and jeers and snide epithets.

Sightless and shorn, at each break of dawn,
Samson-the-husky is grinding out corn.
Around and around, all helpless, forlorn,
He's taunted and ridiculed, scoffed at and scorned.

He pleads to Jehovah, forever in prayer,
For only his strength—never mind hair.
"Give me, O Lord, the strength so to tear
The Philistines' temple apart in the square!"

Jehovah at last heard the moans and the prayers,
So he made a dicker right then and there:
He'd get back his strength but not the long hair.
Samson praises the Lord, despite his despair.

As a child leads the way, we hear Samson say,
"Show me the pillars; the temple's mainstays."
He then stumbles along, distraught and distrait,
As he says to himself, "Every dog has his day."

With that he takes hold of the pillars and shouts,
"You've had it, you Philies, you phonies, you louts!"
As the pillars give way and debris falls about,
The Philistines perish, as does Samson, no doubt.

TANNHÄUSER

Walküre 19

*T*his is the house of the lecherous louse,
The venerable, hoary philosopher Faust.
He's surrounded with skulls, test tubes, and vats,
Ancient parchments, chemicals, dead rats, and bats.

The disgruntled old alchemist, cold misanthropist,
Regrets things of the world and the fleshpots he's missed.
So he calls to the devil to come to his aid.
He'll sell his old soul for youth and a maid.

The devil, who's always alive and alert,
Arrives on the scene, lively and pert.
"*Me voici*," says the devil—in this case he's French.
"At your service, *docteur. Voulez-vous* a young wench?"

"I came when you called, *mon maître*, so speak."
"I'm a skeptic," says Faust, in a tenory squeak.
"I've no need of riches, glory, or fame.
However, you may be of use just the same."

"*Très bien*," says Mephisto. "What would you have, then?"
"A chicken," says Faust, "not an old boiling hen.
I crave young caresses, to tell you the truth;
Something tender and lively in bed. I want youth!"

FAUST

So right then and there, without moving a hair,
A vision of beauty appears in the air.
It's "Gretchen am Spinnrad," the sweet Marguerite,
Turning the wheel with her two dainty feet.

The ancient Lothario falls nearly apart.
The vision's too much for his ancient old heart.
"It's a deal," he tells Satan. "Now what do I do?
The sooner the better. It's all up to you."

"How *gemütlich*," says Faust, the lascivious swine.
"She's right up my alley. *Zo wunderschön—Hein?*"
"Take it easy," says Satan. "Sign your name on that line;
Right on those dots, just below Proserpine's.

"Don't forget what I say; you've the devil to pay;
Of course, not on earth, you old boulevardier.
I'll be within sight, both day and at night,
But down there where I live, your soul's mine—all right?"

He hands Faust a scroll, impish and bold.
Der Herr Doktor signs and forfeits his soul.
Faust then drinks a brew from the devil's own hand.
At once he's turned into a dashing young man.

ACT II – *The Kermesse*

Not even the Breughels could paint such a scene
Of drinking and dancing, with laughter and screams.
There are burghers and students; soldiers and Fraus;
The whole scene's alive; *sehr freundlich*; a WOW!

Amid all this revel appears Valentine,
Marguerite's brother, grave, dull, saturnine.
He's there among soldiers, students, Siebel.
He's going off to war and he's surly as hell.

His one greatest worry is leaving the town
Where his ancestors died, but he can't stick around.
Deutschland über alles. But he begs of his friends,
"Keep an eye on my sister." (She'll need more;
    you'll see when!)

Mephisto appears, full of charm and good cheer;
Distinguished, *soigné*—a real cavalier.
His aim is to please, and he's always at ease.
With devil-may-care, he starts shooting the breeze.

He strikes at a cask that starts pouring wine.
He sneers as the revelers all get in line.
They jump and they bump; it's a real turnverein.
Everyone's merry, except Valentine.

When Lucifer mentions the name Marguerite,
Valenting jumps from his seat to his feet.
"Enough is too much," shrieks the grumpy *soldat*.
"I'll settle his hash right here on the spot."

The imp with his sword makes a ring on the ground.
They start fencing and dancing, around and around.
Valentine's sword is smashed right in two.
He's madder'n hell; the chorus is, too.

Everyone's gauche, but not at a loss.
The men turn their swords, forming a cross.
The devil is cowed, as you may well expect.
He cringes away. That did it, by heck!

With ants in the pants, stirred up in advance,
The overhauled Faust can't wait for romance.
"Take it easy," says Satan. "She's coming this way.
Remember, don't rush, just do as I say."

The sweet Marguerite is walking alone;
Modest and shy, she's on her way home.
Her eyes are cast down like the maiden forlorn
That once milked the cow with the two crumpled horns.

The lustful old boy can hardly stand still.
He rushes the Fräulein without cunning or skill.
Says he, "Fair demoiselle, may I escort you home?"
"*Nein*," replies Marguerite. "I can manage alone."

"You blew it," said Satan. "Though she's not very bright,
Your impatient advance set her afright.
Marguerite, I have found, is not very profound,
But she can tell a pass from a hole in the ground."

"Please leave me," says Faust to Mephistopheles.
"Without you somehow I feel more at ease."
The salacious, remodeled Herr Doktor Faust
Sings a heart-melting song to the dear humble house.

Though he'd like to renege, the devil says, "No.
The die has been cast, and that's how it goes.
Besides, I have brought a case of rare gems;
Just wait till she sees them. You're in, young old man."

The fair Marguerite again enters the scene.
"I wonder," she sighs, "who that guy could have been.
Perhaps he's a knight. And what might be his name?"
She picks up the spindle, reflects, and declaims.

Marguerite then gets up after spinning away
And finds on the door the garden bouquet.
"How sweet of Siebel to pick them for me,"
Then suddenly says, "What's this that I see?"

"A casket of jewels. From whom can they be?
Rhinestones, how brightly they shine," murmurs she.
"I dare not look in, but I'm dying to see."
How could she know it was diablerie?

Meanwhile Mephisto throws Faust the first cue;
With devilish tact tells the guy what to do.
"Take her arm, you dumb cluck" (he means Marguerite's).
"The battle is won. Get going, *tout de suite*."

At first Marguerite acts shy and discreet;
As the hotpot approaches, she tries to retreat.
"Please don't go away," he begs her. "Please stay.
Do you live here alone?" he asks. "Please do say."

She tells him her brother has gone off to war,
Her mother is dead, then goes on some more.
How she lost little sister—an angel was she.
It's all very touching—also touching is he.

He touches her arm; she escapes in alarm.
Then he tells her he loves her, with finesse and charm.
He sounds so convincing, and she is so dumb,
She believes every word. The worst is to come!

Mephisto is mad as the devil can be,
"She was right in the sack, and you let her flee."
But all is not lost. Marguerite reappears.
She opens her window and dreams without fear.

When Maggie's in doubt, she consults marguerites;
Plucks petal by petal so dainty and sweet.
She believes in the message those petals express;
Hers never say no; they always say yes!

"He loves me," she sighs, as she looks toward the sky.
Then all of a sudden she spots Faust and sighs.
She opens the door, only a notch;
Faust enters, but not for a mere kaffeeklatsch.

ACT IV

Pregnant, abandoned, she's left in the lurch.
She's shunned by the faithful as they enter the church.
To make it still worse, she hears demons call,
"Marguerite, you are jilted," they say, one and all.

The soldiers return, triumphant, in line.
Among them is surly and dull Valentine.
The first one he sees is the faithful Siebel.
"Where is my sister?" he asks. "Please, do tell."

"Perhaps she's in church," answers Siebel.
He stumbles for words—how can he tell?
"That's just like Marguerite," then says Valentine.
"For my safe return she's praying. How fine.

But murder will out and sometimes the truth.
Val learns the worst, as the bard says, "Forsooth!"
He has no compassion—that clod, that galoot.
Siebel pleads and begs him have pity, en route.

"Who done it?" he cries. "I'll murder the guy.
He'll pay through the nose. For this he must die."
Mephisto and Faust are back on the scene.
With devil-may-care, Mephistopheles sings.

"What do you here?" bursts forth Valentine.
"Your song's for my sister. Take this, you swine."
Mephisto's guitar he smashes in two,
Then, pointing to Faust, says, "Now I'll settle you."

The medallion that Marguerite gave him one day,
He pulls from his neck and casts it away.
Then, pointing to Faust, says, "*Und Du, schweiner Hund!*"
Both draw swords, and Valentine falls moribund.

The neighbors rush out. Val's drawing a crowd.
With his very last breath he keeps crying out loud
Maledictions, damnations at poor Marguerite,
Who loses her mind and goes nutty *tout de suite*.

ACT V

Marguerite's thrown in jail for infanticide.
In a vision she sees her rejuvenized
Faust, the seducer, the stranger unknown,
Who gallantly offered to escort her home.

The devil—the fiend—and *der Doktor* as well
Have entered, invisible, Marguerite's cell.
In a state of confusion, she's as nutty as can be,
So both Faust and Mephisto urge her to flee.

"The demon," she cries, as her mind she regains.
"I've had it," she screams, wants no *auf Wiedersehen*.
She drops to her knees; to heaven she pleads.
Her cries reach the skies; the saints intervene.

La Traviata

Madamigella Va-le-ry
Gave all for love, but not for free.
She did things that she hadn't ought,
This dear, expensive, French cocotte.

Her name is Violet Valery,
But not a shrinking violet she.
Her brow ain't wet with honest sweat;
She charges guys for what they get.

In the first act—that's based on fact—
Violetta's at a party.
She's light and gay, so *negligé*,
So debonair—so tarty.

She drinks to sin—adulterin'
At the party she is at
With gents that lust—the upper crust—
And *femmes hors de combat*.

She meets a guy who's young and shy,
Who starts to woo the lady.
She falls in love, this turtledove,
Whose past was oh, so shady.

She's overwrought—this gay cocotte—and
Sings, "Love is so much hooey."
But just the same, the dame is game.
Perhaps, "*E forse lui?*"

How can she tell—this demoiselle—
If it's the real McCoy?
After she's stepped—been kept and slept—
With cash-and-carry boys.

She's more than fond, this courtesan,
Of life and fun and sin.
"It's folly to be wise," she sings,
Then leaves it ALL—for him.

But it's too late. The three wise fates
Have put their heads together
And what they've brewed and steamed and
    stewed,
No Violet could weather.

Someone, it seems, has spilled the beans
To stuffy Germont *père*.
He starts right out—the grumpy lout—
To catch them in their lair!

So on the scene—peevish and mean—
Seeks out the Jezebel.
But little did he think he'd find
So cultured a gazelle.

He meets the doll—the femme fatale—
Whose past was oh, so shady.
But he's astound' at what he's found.
Like Edie, she's a lady.

The martinet starts the duet
About his daughter pure and fair;
An angel straight from paradise,
About to get the boot—the air.

The groom's a slob—also a snob.
He'll jilt the bride-to-be.
"'Cause Al's affair," he fumes and swears,
"Would ruin him socially."

We hear her say, "No, no, *jamais*.
Please go. I've done no wrong.
Besides, I'm ill. I'm taking pills.
Doc says it won't be long!"

Mid tears and cries he pleads and sighs;
Assures Vi love is fleeting.
Time wounds all heels—yields lousy deals.
"What then?" he keeps repeating.

Is he surprised—can't believe his eyes—
To read she's sold her property;
To have a home that's not a House and
Live in respectability.

He's heard that tarts have noble hearts
And even more—a soul.
Besides the other things they've got,
They all have hearts of gold.

He proves his point. She'll blow the joint.
She'll pay the piper's price.
We hear her say, "The woman pays."
She'll make the sacrifice!

The father mean is now serene,
Grateful he's made the deal;
"Have a nice day; you'll be okay,"
Then marches on—the heel.

With choking throat Vi writes a note,
"Dear Alfred, please forget.
I thought I loved you, but I don't.
That's how it is, my pet."

As Alfred reads, he starts to seethe.
He's furious and sore.
He'll make her pay. She'll rue the day,
That double-dealing ———!

Deep in despair, he pulls his hair.
His dad again appears,
"Come to my arms, my beamish boy.
Let's get away from here."

It's now, Act Three, and now we see
Violetta at a ball.
Although she flits, she's torn to bits.
She fears there'll be a brawl.

She's with Douphol and that took gall—
An ex-amour—and now
A baronet—bound to protect
The tarnished Violet somehow.

Al, too, is there, hides his despair,
But plans to make a scene.
"Come one and all," tipsy, he calls,
And here he vents his spleen.

"See you this dame? Know you her name?"
"Indeed we do, VIOLETTA."
"Well, after all we did and done,
Behold, she's paid—vendetta."

Then, indiscreet, throws at her feet
The loot he's won at cards.
"Oh, what a gall," cries out Douphol.
"I'll settle this canard!"

Then Violet swoons to Verdian tunes
That melt a heart of stone.
While all her friends gather and bend,
Alfredo mopes alone.

This is the cue: pistols for two,
Or swords, if he likes best.
"We'll meet at dawn, you Satan's spawn."
Douphol says, "Be my guest."

Here once again old dad drops in.
How did the prude get there?
To see the ladies of the House
At Flora's pied-à-terre?

It sounds absurd, but still you've heard
How father's sins visit the kids.
But this may be a double take.
The father visits them instead.

At any rate, dad made a date
Just in time to scourge his son.
"No gent should treat a dame that way,
You popinjay, you jerk, you bum."

"What have I done?" He's overcome.
Alfredo's filled with shame, despair.
Too late he learns she loves him still.
He's torn to bits. He leaves with *père*.

It's now Act Four. Vi's at death's door.
She knows the end is near.
"Good-bye," she sighs, for days gone by,
Also to her career.

Her doctor friend tries hope to lend.
He tells her she'll get better.
But it's too late. Those hags, the fates,
Are on their way to get 'er.

From 'twixt her breasts a note she wrests.
She's read it o'er and o'er.
"Forgive our trespasses," it says.
It's from the prude—the genitor.

"You've kept your word, Alfred has heard.
The duel took place at dawn.
Take care. Sit tight. You'll be all right.
We're on our way. *Bon chance.*
        GERMONT."

"Too late," she cries and wipes her eyes.
"*Addio.* Good-bye. Farewell.
Oh, happy days. Oh, sultry nights.
Good-bye, my clientele.

"Oh, joy supreme," we hear her scream,
"Alfredo!" In he flies.
It won't be long. Soon she'll be strong.
All wrongs he'll rectify.

Oh, joy. Oh, glee. They'll leave Paree.
Her health he'll soon restore.
She starts to cough. The trip is off.
She sinks unto the floor.

Before she dies, mid sad good-byes,
She gives her love her effigy,
That he may think of her sometime
While playing with some chickadee.

She's never out of breath, it seems,
Tubercular though she may be;
Sings forte and pianissimos
And gets right up to B.

"In heaven above," she tells her love,
While bitter tears are flowing,
"I'll pray for you." She has no doubt
That's where—nonstop—she's going.

It won't be long. It's her last song.
They'll meet again, but when?
Al knows his dove will fly above
Like the repentant Magdalen.

Henry the Eighth, obnoxious malign,
Became King of England in fifteen 'o nine.
One can see in the portrait of the younger Holbein
The evil innate on the face of that swine.
Brave knights and kings wore tight-fitting pants,
Armor and steel with adamant ants.
Bathroom facilities in those days were tough,
So one made the best with less than enough.

Isabella and Ferdinand, those mad sovereigns of Spain,
Were both psychopathic, deranged, and insane.
With the mad Torquemada, evil, vile, inhumane,
They started that cruel Inquisition of Spain.
Nothing thrilled them so much as an *Auto de Fe*.
They both fervently prayed, as their prey burned away.
The screams of despair that rented the air
Was *Gloria en Excelsis* to that fanatic pair.

The Jews and "heretics" were all dispossessed.
Of what use was wealth to a soul that's possessed?
Catherine of Aragon, that bigot supreme,
Was palmed off to Hank's brother—a political scheme.
This marriage was not consummated, it's claimed.
He was sick, apathetic, so untouched she remained.
One day Henry's brother conveniently died,
So Hank married Catherine, the dear defunct's bride.

Anna Bolena

She had babies nonstop, but all of them died,
Except Bloody Mary, who should not have survived.
Catherine was a bigot, like her mother and dad,
But she couldn't please Henry, nor stir his gonads.
Meanwhile King Henry fell madly in love
With Kate's lady-in-waiting, a sly turtledove.
Anne Boleyn was the name of this designing dame.
She was coy. She was gay. She enticed and inflamed.

She played her cards well. Anne Boleyn was not shy.
She succeeded with wiles to enrapture the guy.
For a crown on her head she told Henry she might,
But for less than a crown she said, "No, not tonight."
When a guy is in heat, he is seldom discreet,
So he promised the crown as he knelt at her feet.
After that Anne was glad to give—tit for tat.
She gave him a sample, and that settled that.

Hank, of course, thought it was all in the bag.
However, the king reached a Vatican snag.
He asked Pope Clement to grant him a divorce.
The Pope said, "You're nuts," and denied it, of course.
"It's against Holy Church," said His Most Holiness,
"But where there's a will, there's a way," he said with finesse.
Henry said to the Pope, "You'll regret it, you dope."
So he started to scheme, refused to give up hope.

Hank decided to start a church of his own,
Be the whole cheese himself—independent of Rome.
If Luther could do it, I can do it too.
Just what has he done that I can't do too?
The rest you all know, how that obese so-and-so
Told the Pontiff to shove it, and gave Rome the last blow.
He got rid of drab Catherine, the bigoted wren,
Then immediately married his adored Anne Boleyn.

Anne gave birth to a girl, which drove Henry mad.
He screamed and he swore like a miserable cad.
Anne got pregnant again—this time 'twas a male,
Born dead! Henry shrieked, cursed, and bewailed.
He had had it with Anne. Her fate was thus sealed.
She was sent to the Tower by that lecherous heel.
"I must have an heir," he fumed and he swore.
Then fell madly in love with shy Jane Seymour.

Accused of adultery, false witness he found.
He had had it with Anne. On her death he was bound.
Lovers, accusers, were indicted abused.
Her own brother of incest he basely accused.
Put to the torture they screamed—writhed in pain.
They "confessed" to escape this scourge inhumane.
They admitted a guilt false and untrue
When put to the rack, pincers, and screws.

Too late they recanted when led to the block.
They were scorned and derided by the mob at the dock.
The accused were menaced, threatened, coerced,
So Anne went to the block, despised and accursed.
Abandoned and scorned by her infamous kin,
Who witnessed against her, to save their own skin.
The whole accusation was framed up by Hank,
Corrupt, syphilitic, repulsive, and rank.

The rest of the murders of Henry the Eighth
Are a matter of history too long to relate.
He lived on to commit horrors and strife;
Also planned to behead Katherine Parr, his sixth wife.
But the monster died shortly—putrid in bed,
And Katherine was able to keep on her head.
He passed on unsung, unwept, and unmourned.
"Good riddance," all cried, but his evil lives on.

Peking. In Fabled Times.

TURANDOT

Behold Turandot, inflexible, taut,
A Chinese virago or worse, it is said.
Before one can jump in her sacrosanct bed,
One must guess three riddles or off goes his head!

To fiddle and diddle with Turandot's riddle
One must be mature and very cocksure.
A dragon is tame compared to this dame,
This almond-eyed vampire, cold, hard, and dour.

Most brave defunct suitors were ardent but small,
But very well hung on the wall are the heads.
So when sex rears its head, no matter what's said,
If you can't guess her riddle, forget about bed.

From far and from near came brave cavaliers
In search of delights and joy epicine;
Mandarins, emirs, caliphs, and peers
Greedy, but not for her Chinese cuisine.

Ping, Pang, and Pong, three boys from a Tong,
Butt in and butt out, obstructing the theme
With tedious quips, facetious and flip,
Disturbing this lurid, murderous scene.

They prance and they dance and make faces.
They think they're the life of the party.
But most of the time give pain in behind,
With Chinese *commedia dell'arte*.

They say heads must fall, like leaves in the fall.
'Tis written in old Chinese tablets and scrolls.
The year of the mouse, the tiger, the louse
Would make the red queen want to crawl in a hole.

Ping yearns for his little gray home in the West.
The other two also grumble and stew:
Pang for his forest in gloomy T'siang;
Pong for his garden of punk and bamboo.

The bloodthirsty crowd is gay, wild, and loud.
They cry for more blood in wild ecstasy.
"Sharpen the knife," they scream with delight.
Death can be fun. Just try it and see.

A voice with a sob cries, "Help," to the mob.
It's the self-sacrificing, charitable Liù.
Her companion is old, feeble, and blind.
They have wandered for days, abused and pursued.

The venerable sire is about to expire,
Crushed by the mob. But a gallant unknown
Comes to the rescue, saves the old man,
As the rabble continues to fume and to foam.

As the prince contemplates, he's amazed, insensate.
The old guy's familiar, but he isn't quite sure.
Then he screams out with joy. It is the old boy,
The old deposed king, his father, Timur.

Their joy is cut short. They must be on guard.
Spies and informers abound everywhere.
He begs them not to say his name and exclaims,
"Remain incognito, I warn you. Beware!"

Timur tells his son of Liù's generous soul;
How she begged for his bread; and deeds unforetold,
Like drying his tears and calming his fears.
"How nice," says the prince, bored and controlled.

Regardless of plots, the prince has the hots,
And with luck he will make the cold Peking duck.
She's hard to ensnare, this cold Frigidaire.
Let 'em all run amuck; he trusts in chuck-luck.

The bloodthirsty mob keeps screaming for blood,
When all of a sudden the Ming doll appears.
She's all gussied up with tinsel and stuff,
While the mob of the slobs falls in trembling fear.

She raises her hand from the perch where she stands,
Encouraging slaughter of heads more and more.
She warns horny studs, they'll pay with their blood,
Then proceeds with her story of horror and gore.

The caliph's bewitched by this dazzling witch.
All warnings he shuns, ignores, and rejects.
Although it's forbade, he'll get to her pad.
Come heaven or hell, he'll vanquish the hex.

"Okay, feisty stranger. Have it your way,"
She sneers and she jeers. "Now we'll see, you poor dope.
What's born every day and dies every night?"
In ecstatic joy, the prince says, "Hope."

In rage, fear, and scorn, the princess replies,
"Tell me, smart guy, what's like flame and not fire?"
"Blood," says the prince, without even a wince;
And here Turandot almost expires.

She steps down the stairs with scorn and despair.
The passionate prince falls on his knees.
She looks down with scorn at his masculine form,
As the mob sinks to the ground solemnly.

Here the venerable emperor appears in the clouds.
As the mob shrieks with joy in frenzied acclaim,
"Hail, venerable Son of Heaven," they yell.
"Live ten thousand years in honor and fame."

His name is Altoum and he looks disentombed.
The old gink will be lucky if he lasts through the night.
"Live ten thousand years," the mob bellows and cheers.
In a weak voice he begs the prince to take flight.

Distraught, Turandot starts descending the stairs.
Grimly she asks, "What's like ice and not fire?"
"My fire will melt your fire—TURANDOT!"
It's correct, and again she almost expires.

"Celestial Father," she cries in despair.
"Release me. Revoke this oath, I implore.
Throw not your daughter in this stranger's arms.
Cast not a smirch on our blessed ancestors!"

"Who is this unknown?" they shriek, wild, untamed.
"His name," yells the mob, rabid, insane.
Already the prince has forbidden Timur
And also the slave girl to utter his name.

The slave girl is tortured, manhandled, and scourged.
His father is crushed by the mad hangman's heel.
The caliph looks on, unstirred and untouched,
Delighted his name has not been revealed.

Liù pleads with the prince to speak out his name.
He lends a deaf ear to her supplicant plea,
Begs her stop weeping, and go on her way.
"And by the way, Liù. Take daddy too, please."

For love, little Liù sacrifices her life,
Stabs herself in the heart, and dies at his feet.
"How nice of dear Liù not to mention my name.
The dear little thing indeed was discreet."

The frigid enchantress steps to the ground,
Grim, and determined he'll not get his way.
And although the riddles were answered and solved,
She'll fight to the end to keep him out of the hay.

He offers a deal to this woman of steel.
He'll be willing to die if she guesses his name.
The deal is a flop, so the prince, chop-chop,
Tears the veil from her face and conquers the dame.

Oh, heavenly bliss. To think what she missed,
This sinister, coy, cloisonné turtledove.
After death and destruction, torture and pain,
These two schizophrenics declare, "It is love."

And so ends the story, lurid and gory,
Of gonads and hormones, alas and alack.
But, no doubt they'll have fun, those two maniacs,
Wondering who's more impressed in and out of the sack.

Mantua. Sixteenth Century.
ACT I, SCENE I

Not even a gaucho could have been more macho
Than Gualtier Maldé, the duke, as you'll see.
After doing girls wrong, he'd burst into song,
Singing "Women are fickle," the debauched licensee.

The women he found could be all pushed around,
So he shoved them on couches, sofas, and beds.
He abducted, seduced, Monterone's *jeune fille*,
And the sly Rigoletto laughed off his head.

"Laugh, you old rake, you poisonous snake,"
Cried Monterone, a father bereft.
"I curse you, vile serpent. Blood be on your head."
With this malediction, old Monterone left.

Shocked, stunned, and appalled, consumed in his gall,
The court jester's leer froze on his face;
Perplexed, at a loss, made the sign of the cross,
Then solemnly left, in a slow, measured pace.

Rigoletto grows worse, brooding over the curse
Hurled at his head by the Count Monterone.
He worries and frets for his daughter, his pet,
Who lives with a daft, irresponsible crone.

RIGOLETTO

As he mopes like a churl o'er the fate of his girl,
He's approached by a brigand, a killer, a thug.
He stops Rigoletto in front of his house,
Whispers, "Be on your guard, you're surrounded by mugs.

"I'm Sparafucile, better known as the heel.
I liberate folks from whoever it be.
I save, for a price, folks from danger and strife.
I deliver a creep, defunct, COD.

"I've a beautiful sister; no man can resist her.
She gives me a hand to lure men, understand?
I might add if perchance, you've no cash on hand,
We'll bump someone off on the installment plan."

"So you work with your gun," said the jester. "What fun!
My weapon's my tongue, more potent, you bum.
Leave your name and address, and in case I'm harassed,
I'll give you a call, you Burgundian scum!"

SCENE 2 – *Rigoletto's Dwelling*

After leaving the louse, he enters his house.
Gilda flies to his arms with cadenzas galore,
Then with more *fioriture*, staccato, bravuras,
She asks her dad questions he more than deplores.

"Speak, daddy, do, just one word or two.
Tell me vis-à-vis about our family tree.
I know it's a subject that pains you indeed,
But I'd like to know who mother was, please."

"I'd rather not say, at least not today.
Speak not of that, angel, but let's just chat."
Then avoiding all questions about pedigree,
He tells her her mother is dead and that's that.

Gilda then tells her dad she's contented and glad,
So she goes straight to church after leaving the house,
But she did not confess that she met after mass
A student, who said he was poor as a mouse.

"Gracious maid," said the guy, the wolf in disguise,
"Allow if I may present myself, pray.
I'm a poor, humble student. I'm Gualtier Maldé.
Please, may I walk you home? I'm going your way."

The gullible Gilda accepts with delight.
In the courtyard the duke swears love evermore.
Ecstatic, enraptured, she falls for his line
Then tells him to scram, the old man's near the door.

"*Caro nome*," she sings; with *bel canto* it rings.
She could not efface the name from her head;
She trilled like a bird, every phrase, every word;
Then picked up her lantern and went straight to bed.

We are still in the road where Gilda abodes,
And what's this we see, courtiers by the score.
They plan to abduct for a joke and a laugh
The gal they suspect is the old jester's whore.

Rigoletto appears and starts trembling with fear
As he finds the courtiers in front of his house.
But they deftly explain that they're playing a game
To abduct from next door their own comrade's spouse.

With masks and with cloaks for this practical joke,
The nefarious group set to work on the task.
"Let me in on the spree," says the jester in glee.
"And since you're all disguised, give me, too, a mask."

It's hard to believe he could be so deceived,
But this plot is chuck full of such tommyrot.
They convince the poor dolt the ladder to hold.
(This is Piave's libretto, believe it or not.)

The kidnap takes place, sardonic and base.
'Mid screams of despair, away Gilda's led.
For bad or for worse, old Monterone's curse
Relentlessly falls on the old jester's head.

ACT II – *Hall in the Palace*

The heartless courtiers, unscrupulous peers,
Concealed in the palace the abducted girl,
Derided the clown, pushed and kicked him around,
Rigoletto's despair was a laugh in their world.

With a smile on each face, the rakes sought His Grace;
Told the duke they'd abducted the old jester's broad.
"We'd suspected the jester of hiding a love,
A benign concubine," laughed the conspirators.

The duke smelled a rat; thought could it be that
His jolly courtiers had made a mistake;
That he'd find in his lair the maiden so fair,
Gilda, his prey? Oh, boy. What a break.

When the scheming young duke discovered the fluke
And found he'd been duped by his own sycophants,
He stopped being jocose, said they'd pay through the nose;
He'd give all those jokers a kick in the pants.

He seeks and he finds his love in a bind,
Concealed in the palace, misused and rebuked.
She falls in his arms in tears and alarm.
She then is seduced by the inconstant duke.

Needless to say, the duke got his way.
She gave him her all with love in her heart.
It's a *femme*'s whole existence, the sages do say.
It was fiddle-de-dee with the duke from the start.

Disheveled, dismayed, seduced, and betrayed,
Gilda rushes and drops at the old jester's feet;
Then in misery and pain confesses her shame,
As he comforts his daughter in anguished defeat.

In frenzied despair, pulling his hair,
The heartbroken jester starts playing it cool,
Concealing his pain, pretending a game,
Does a "laugh, clown, laugh" act in a cold court of fools.

Monterone reappears under guard, and he sneers
As he points at the portrait that hangs on the wall.
"Though I cursed you, vile duke, you live after all.
Your sins go unpunished; you live after all."

"Old man, you are wrong, and it will not be long.
You'll soon be avenged," the jester replies.
Then addressing the portrait, he vents out his spleen.
"Vendetta, tremenda vendetta," he cries.

ACT III – *Sparafucile's Duplex*

The jester's hell-bent to avenge with revenge
His daughter, betrayed by His Highness, the skunk.
He'll pay with his life, with the thrust of a knife,
And die like a fly, the philandering punk.

Although Gilda mopes over the dope,
She can't be convinced her lover's a heel.
Rigoletto will prove that the duke is a churl.
A scoundrel, deceiver, a slippery eel.

The deal has been made; the killer half paid.
The seducing malfactor will get what he gets.
The evening is rife with murder and strife,
With nothing in sight but the thrilling quartet.

They arrive in despair at the crook's pied-à-terre.
Gilda is led to the murderer's lair.
She trembles with fear. She listens and hears
"*La donna è mobile*," that old hackneyed air.

"Come here, Gilda dear. Lend an eye and an ear.
Stand here and listen and look through the crack."
In terror and fear she looks and she hears
That mundane seducer, that sex maniac.

Maddalena, the slut, accustomed to smut,
Kids the duke, more or less, but falls for his rot.
Believe it or not she's touched to the heart,
Or rather he touched a more vulnerable spot.

She fell for the swine hook, sinker, and line,
Begged her brother, the killer, to spare the signor.
The assassin agrees, in terms such as these,
To kill the first man that knocks at their door.

Gilda heard what they said, and although her heart bled,
She'll give up her life for the man she adores.
She was glad daddy dear was not near to hear
The evil complot of the crook and the whore.

To Gilda the father said, "Go on ahead.
Get a horse and return disguised as a man.
When my task is complete, we'll blow this retreat
And rush to Verona as fast as we can."

Attired in men's clothes, as a metamorphose,
Gilda quickly returns to the murderer's shack.
She knocks quite discreet, softly says, "Trick or treat?"
They open the door and she's stabbed in the back.

Rigoletto returns to settle the terms;
Paid the rest of the dough to the murdering thief;
Took the sack on his back, ecstatic with joy;
Contented, starts off with revengeful relief.

"Do please allow me," said the killer with glee,
"To throw the sack in the river. Our aim is to please.
We call and deliver, right into the river.
I'll throw the sack in with pleasure and ease."

With joy and dispatch, the clown opens the sack,
"Ye gods. Am I mad? I'm losing my head."
He discovers his Gilda, breathing her last,
Mortally stabbed by the killer, who fled.

"Oh, Gilda, my loved one," he moans and he cries
As Gilda reacts and sings from the sack,
"In heaven with mamma, we'll pray for you, dear."
With that she expires, alas and alack.

DAS RHEINGOLD

Voglinde, Welgunde and Floshilde too
Are three naughty Rhinemaidens, between me and you.
They swim rivers and seas, singing German shanties.
In their hair they wear seaweeds and anemones.
They are thoroughly *femme*. Don't care about men.
They've said time and again, "We can live without them!

"We have marvelous times with the fish in the Rhine,
So why bother with men? They're a bore most of the time!"
They ride the seahorses—they're the Rhine's taxicabs.
They hobnob with lobsters, and joke with cracked crabs.
They nurse motherless eels and lost baby seals.
With devotion and love, they feed them their meals.

Albrecht the gnome lives down deep in the Rhine.
He gets *mal de Mer*, way down in the slime.
He comes up for air many a time
To gaze at the Rhinemaids, with evil design.
In the bottomless pit he's the big *maitre d'*.
But the Rhinemaids make sport of him, as you'll see.

As Albrecht one day came up from the brine,
A Rhinemaid winked, a most immoral Eve.
That rickety dwarf felt encouraged, of course.
So he tried to capture one of them by force.
She laughed at him tauntingly, snickered and jeered.
But the deluded runt thought that she was sincere.

Despite the gods' warning to guard the Rhinegold,
They paid no attention to what they'd foretold.
They told the old gnome that he could own the world.
But he'd have to live life without love—without girls.
The maids thought they'd put the gnome in his place,
Not suspecting that Albrecht was holding an ace.

The Rhinemaids believed that by pulling that stunt,
The world and its gold wouldn't interest the runt.
Then they tauntingly said, if he'd fashion a ring
From the Rhinegold, he'd become rich as a king.
But the leering Rhinemaids this time got fooled.
Money CAN buy love, thought the scheming old ghoul.

He snatched the Rhinegold, then scooted away
And fiendishly sneered, "Every dog has his day."
He hooted and howled as he dove down the Rhine.
Said, "'Laughs best who laughs last,' mein Lieber Freulines."
Now we go to Walhalla, on a great mountaintop,
The home of the gods is just one simple hop.

Wotan and Fricka are fast asleep, snoring.
Fricka wakes up. It's late in the morning.
She pokes Wotan and says, "Wake up, dunderhead.
The giants are coming. We're in trouble," she said.
"You know well, Mein Herr Wotan, those giants want
    their pay.
They want Freya, not me, I'm sorry to say!

"That apple of Freya's contains alchemy.
So go warn that frump goddess of their cupidity.
They want to stay young, those heavyweight bums.
That apple can do it and they know it—that scum.
Freya doesn't mind being treated real rough.
After all, she knows giants are really hot stuff.

"And why shouldn't Fafner and Fasolt get paid,
Since Freya might enjoy a roll in the hay?"
Here Albrecht appears, crows that he made the ring
From the gold from the Rhine, and are they chagrined.
Fafner and Fasolt snatch Freya away,
And will not release her unless Wotan pays.

But they got their comeuppance. The giants lost their youth.
And Freya is more than disgusted—"forsooth."
"The giants lost more than their youth, by the way,"
Said Freya, disgruntled. "I think they're all gay!"
Wotan worries and schemes how to retrieve the ring
Made from the Rhinegold the Rhinemaids gave that gink.

That vile little dwarf works the Nebelungs to death,
From morning to night, to their very last breath.
Mime's the village blacksmith down there.
He's Albrecht's brother, and mean as a bear.
He forged a gold helmet and, strange as it seems,
Who wears it cannot be distinguished or seen.

The helmet has power to change human beings
Into dragons or toads or other vile things.
With the ring there is nothing Albrecht can't do.
He can change to a dragon or a slimy toad too.
The god Loge guides Wotan to regions below,
Whereupon Wotan crushes a toad with his toe.

The toad was Albrecht, in case you don't know—
Albrecht the gnome incognito.
The helmet was rushed by Loge to Earth.
They also grabbed Albrecht, that monstrous squirt.
They refused to release him until he gave back
The ring and the helmet and the bric'brac.

Albrecht is frantic. He swears and declares
The ring will bring death to whomever it wears.
The giants pile the helmet and the gold in a heap.
But Wotan refuses the ring to those creeps.
Erda the earthworm creeps up from the earth.
Predicts doom and destruction to Wotan, and worse!

Strange as it seems, Wotan falls fast asleep.
Wakes up in a tizzy, throws the ring at those creeps.
The fling of the ring frees Freya, it seems.
She makes her escape from those heavyweight fiends.
Mealy-mouth Wotan begins getting disturbed.
He's listened to Erda and believes every word.

As Wotan's admiring the magical ring,
The giants are back again, evil and grim.
They demand that Freya be covered with gold.
In a Christian Dior gown she must be enfold.
But they must leave an opening, or at least a hole,
To stick in the ring, the gods are thus told.

The gods yell and scream. They say they will not.
So again Freya's carried off, there on the spot.
Dirty Erda creeps up from the earth once again.
Starts all over again to gripe and complain.
"Stop being perverse. The ring is accursed.
Get with it, *dummkopf*, or things will get worse."

"Okay," said Wotan, "I'll do as you say.
No use arguing with women." Throws the ring away.
The ring strikes Fasolt, who's killed on the spot
By Fafner, his buddy, believe it or not.
Wotan decides to go back to Walhalla
On a rainbow bridge made by the thunder god Donner.

Too late the Rhinemaidens cry, weep, and whine.
Their laments can be heard coming up from the Rhine.
The Rhinemaids too late realize they've been bilked,
So keep wailing and weeping over spilt milk.
They continue to bawl and howl uncontrolled,
Even after the curtain falls on *Das Rheingold*.

The Trojans

Cavalleria Rusticana

Madame Butterfly

Act I

*D*o come with me across the sea
To dear old Nagasaki.
Meet Cio-Cio-San, pride of Japan,
And drink her health with saki.

From the U.S.A. one fine day
Arrived the U.S. Navy;
With it, a Yank with stripes and rank.
He rikee misbehavey.

He meet'em man with fix'em plan
To marry Japan rady.
Yank say okay; he give'em pay.
Broker bow deep. He shady!

With quaint allure, shy and demure,
With parasol and fan,
She makes her way across the bay,
Enchanting Cio-Cio-San.

"Oh, happy day," everyone say.
"*Bonzai* to Yankee man."
Bend very low. Walk on tiptoe.
Play tune on samisen.

But what is this—this noise, this hiss?
Across the bridge he comes;
Screaming a curse, abuse, and worse,
The fuming Uncle Bonze.

"You faithress one. What have you done?"
He points to Cio-Cio-San.
"You cast'em smirch on Shinto church.
You marry 'Merican."

"Get out, get out," the Yank cries out,
"You prancing marionette.
Karate you, that's what I'll do.
I'll teach you etiquette."

Then one by one, sulky and glum,
The guests follow the priest.
They scorn and shun poor Butterfly
And leave the wedding feast.

Rieutenant say, "All go away."
He very nice; he Yankee.
He carry Cio-Cio-San inside;
Then both make hanky-panky.

Then one fine day, he go away
But promise come back soon,
When robin redbreast making nest
And cherry brossom broom.

Act II

Three years go by, and Butterfly,
She wait and wait and wait.
Three times red robin making nest,
But Pinkerton, he late.

Then by and by another guy.
Rich man name Yamadori,
He rikee marry Butterfly;
Got yen. He hunky-dory.

Then consul guy come back and try
To reading bridegroom note
Terring about a Yankee bride
Coming with him on boat.

With great fatigue he starts to read.
She stumps him from the start.
He just can't make her realize
She's jilted, so departs.

Her faithful maid comes to her aid.
"You marry Yamadori.
He ugly so, but he got dough."
But Cio-Cio-San ignoring.

Suzuki say, another day,
"You marry rich man maybe?"
"Oh, no, me Missi Pinkerton.
Me marry. Me have baby."

Poor Butterfly, she start to cry.
Suzuki crying, too.
"Don't cry," say Madame Butterfly.
"Groom come. I promise you."

"Me not tell joke. Soon you see smoke
Coming from boat from sea."
Then Butterfly say, "Listen why,"
And start to singing "*Un bel di.*"

Then pretty soon, hearing big boom,
Big boat arrive in port.
"You see?" say Madame Butterfly.
Suzuki only making snort.

So here and there and everywhere
Brossom and cherry broom—
Across the floor, in front of door—
To welcome Yankee groom.

Then all night long, waiting till dawn,
Making big hole in screen;
Looking with hope, with telescope,
For husband from Marine.

At break of day, Suzuki say,
"You up all night; preese rest.
I call you when he come," she say,
Then make kabuki face, depressed.

Alas, alack, he did come back.
But not alone—the heel.
His blushing bride is by his side;
Her name is Kate—so shy, genteel.

"Ah, woe is me. What do I see?
My heart is torn with pain."
Too touched to face poor Butterfly,
He sneaks away again.

Butterfly soon, rushing in room,
Thinking he's come—her mate.
He came all right but got uptight,
So he passed the buck to Kate.

"Who is this dame? Preese, why you came?
What for you in my house?"
She learns the worse—the Shinto curse.
The lady is his spouse!

To make things worse and more perverse
Kate hangs around awhile;
Then blithely asks poor Butterfly
If they might take the child.

And Butterfly—she does not cry—
Just say, "Come back for baby soon."
She knows alas that all is past;
The Shinto curse has sealed her doom.

Yes, Butterfly say she must die,
So she make hara-kiri.
Everyone cry; not one seat dry;
All people feeling teary.

Curtain come down. No one make sound.
Then Butterfly come back;
Making big bow; throwing kiss, kowtow.
Everyone crap, crap, crap.

Act I

*O*roveso, the chief of the Druids, appears,
Crying, "War on the Romans!" 'mid bravos and cheers.
At the rise of the moon, Norma whacks off a hunk
Of the sacrosanct mistletoe, Druidical bunk!

Norma's a priestess and daughter as well
Of the High Priest Or'veso, who's rabid as hell.
She tells the belligerents, the wild guttersnipes,
The time to attack is not yet quite ripe.

What she doesn't tell dad or the wild Druid mob
Is the fact that she married an enemy slob.
She also conceals that she broke sacred vows
And bore him two kids, but she does it somehow.

She hoodwinks the Druids with subtle mystique,
Thus saving the life of her husband (the sneak).
She then sings a hymn to her goddess, the moon,
Praising chastity, virtue, and rays she has strewn.

The jerk Norma wed is a slick Roman heel,
A philandering Latin, a slippery eel.
For his wife and the kids he couldn't care less;
He loves Adalgisa, another priestess.

Adalgisa's a Druid vestal—and how!
The world and the flesh she renounced, took the vows.
Then Pollione appears (by the way, that's his name).
She falls for his line, but to err is humane.

"Adalgisa," he begged, "come with me to Rome.
Why hang around with these drips 'round the throne?
I'll swear love eternal if you'll just fly away
To a civilized land. Love, live, and (oh) lay!"

Adalgisa, when priestess, worked magic rites, too;
Was clairvoyant and psychic, this everyone knew;
Cast horoscopes, too, for the Druids of Gaul;
Read tea leaves, and gazed into round crystal balls!

But the tea leaves and stars failed to reveal
That her proconsul wolf was a real Roman heel.
He'd break ties with Norma, his legal-wed spouse,
Leave wife, home, and children, that two-timing louse!

Adalgisa knew Norma did, too, break her vow;
Kept marriage and kids a dark secret somehow.
Adalgisa confesses her guilt to her friend;
Norma absolves her and abjures help to lend.

"Do tell me," asks Norma, "the name of the guy,"
When enters Pollione, contrite, shy, and sly.
"Don't tell me it's him (or "he," as it were)!"
She started to curse, called him, "You lousy cur!

Come away from that tree, you two-timing skunk.
You'll pay through the nose, you adulterous punk!"
Her screams, maledictions reached clear to the sky.
She then picked up a pot to clobber the guy.

He ducked just in time, then jumped, leaped, and ran,
Disgusted that Norma did not understand.
But hell hath no fury like a woman who's scorned.
By her gods she did swear he'd regret he was borned.

How could Adalgisa have known it was he,
The husband of Norma? So nonplussed was she,
She couldn't believe she had been so deceived;
Swore to give him the air. (Can this be believed?)

ACT II, SCENE 1

We're in Norma's abode in the forest somewhere.
She enters with dagger, distraught, in despair.
She swore he would pay, that two-timing rat.
She'd have her revenge by slaying his brats.

Adalgisa arrives just barely in time
To stop her dear friend from committing a crime.
"If Medea could do it to Jason, that swine,
What's to stop *me?*" asks Norma, defiant, malign.

"Oh, hear me, dear Norma, pray don't be so rash.
He doesn't deserve it, that low Roman trash.
Do think it over, I beg of you, please.
Just look at those cherubs asleep by your knees!"

For Norma, these words touched her motherly heart,
Adalgisa then takes both the kids and departs.
Forsaken, rejected, Norma moans and she cries,
"I was false to my vows and for this I must die!"

SCENE 2

We're back in the grove among the oak trees.
Norma's still filled with vengeance no soul can appease.
Her Virgo's conjunct with Saturn and Mars,
Which forebodes hanky-panky, said her wise avatar.

"And I thought," cries out Norma, "my chum was a brick.
But she hands me the dirty end of the stick.
That bunk about hoping to retake her vow,
That's bull and baloney. I know it, and how!"

Norma's told that Pollione is hot on the trail
Of his love Adalgisa, and this time won't fail.
He'll snatch her away from her false Druid gods
And fly back to Rome, despite all the odds.

"Oh, yeah?" cries out Norma. "That's what *he* thinks!
I'll show him what's what, that vile Roman fink!"
She flies to the altar and thrice strikes the shield,
Which means war-to-the-finish of those Roman
    "schlemiels."

Oroveso, the Druids, the whole mob appears,
All armed to the teeth with picks, swords, and spears.
"The altar, the gods have all been defiled."
Norma screams, "Bring Pollione and prepare the pile!"

They bring in Pollione. The Druids scream, "Boo!"
Oroveso starts raising a hullabaloo!
"Whom do I see?" cries Pollione, surprised.
"Wow!" It's Norma, his mate, with fire in her eyes.

"Kill him!" the Druids scream, yell, and shriek.
Norma goes to him; then trembles, grows weak.
She offers an out to the grand prix de Rome:
"Dump Adalgisa for good and then come on home!"

"I'll pursue her," he swears, "and drag her to Rome.
I'll knock down your idol, that fraud made of stone!
Else, hand me the dagger, I'll take my own life,
But spare Adalgisa more sorrow and strife!"

"Listen," says Norma, "you vile, faithless thug.
Adalgisa will perish unpitied, you slug.
Through her I'll get even with you, have no doubt.
She'll pay for your sins, you fatheaded lout!

"She sullied the altar, the Druids, our god,
Forsook her own vows, Irmansul's sacred rod."
Norma then cries for vengeance; her final appeal.
She'll denounce the false priestess; her doom thus is sealed.

"Her name!" cries the mob, now eager for gore.
And curses upon her they shriek and they roar.
"The culprit am I!" Norma cries in dismay.
"For my crimes and dishonor, 'tis I that must pay!"

The Druids are shocked, one and all supplicate.
"Recant!" they beseech her. "Deny! Exculpate!"
She reveals she's a mother, to Oroveso, her dad;
Begs him care for her two beloved, guiltless lads.

The mob turns again and "Curses!" they cry,
And "Off with her wreath! Let the vile sinner die!"
Pollione's love is rekindled. For his sins he'll atone.
He vows he'll die with her; she'll not die alone.

Repentant, chagrined, and weary of life,
Pollione refalls in love with his wife.
Refilled with desire, he ponders the pyre.
He's yearning to burn with his spouse in the fire.

Together they step with hands holding hands
To the funeral pyre, toward the bright-flaming brands.
Our hearts break for Norma. We sob and we cry.
But flames never killed a worthier guy.

The Girl of the Golden West

This is a tale of muck and kale;
Of lust and raw, red liquor;
Of miners bold, who kill for gold,
Without an eyelash flicker.

Minnie's the star. She runs a bar;
Also a doggie diner.
And though men swear, kill, and ensnare,
She could not be refiner.

All tough as stakes, these mining rakes,
Steeped to their necks in sin;
Hard-boiled, uncouth, tough, vulgar sleuths,
Yet one and all love Min.

Dear Min's a virgin, chaste and pure,
And like the blessed demoiselle,
She, too, leans far across the bar,
Whiskey, wines, and beer she sells.

A traveling minstrel wanders in
And starts to sing "Old Folks at Home."
Those buccaneers and racketeers
Shed maudlin tears in beer afoam.

Between the booze that flows profuse,
The shooting, and the lust,
Min reads the Bible to those thugs,
Though not one is abstemious.

"There is no sin," she says to them,
"That cannot find redemption,
Providing boys like you repent
Of things not fit to mention."

But that's a fact—Min's kept intact—
Has not been touched by human hands;
Until Dick Johnson came around
And stunned her with a meaning glance.

Dick Johnson is his nom de plume,
Or nom de crook, if you prefer;
A swindler come to raid and rob,
A dangerous adventurer.

Now Sheriff Rance, he's got hot pants
For Minnie, virginal and sweet;
Declares his love, by stars above;
But gets the air *tout de suite*.

Min turns him down. He spits and frowns.
"I'll get you yet, proud beauty.
My love you spurn, but I'll return";
Then goes off to his duty.

Here Dick comes in; gazes at Min.
He's startled and, what's more,
He says, "Your face is familiar.
Haven't we met someplace before?

"Yes, I remember now," says Dick.
"'Twas in the camp," he says, entranced.
"Yes," blushes Min, "you *do* recall."
He's listening in, the rat, Jack Rance.

"We don't like strangers hanging 'round,
And what's your name, I'd like to know?"
"It's Johnson." "And what else?" asks Rance.
"I'm Johnson from Sacramento."

Here Rance draws back in quite a huff.
The green-eyed monster's got him down.
He sneers and jeers and sweats and fumes
And evern worse now Dick's in town.

Meanwhile there is a tete-à-tete,
As Min and Johnson chat and smile.
They're getting on magnificently,
Recalling where they've met erstwhile.

The big, bad wolf butts in again;
"Look here, you, from Sacramento.
What is your business here in town?
I'm Sheriff Rance, 'case you don't know."

"Lay off," says Min. "I'll vouch for him.
Now run along. Please do."
In stifled rage, Rance leaves the bar,
While Min and Johnson start anew.

And now there is a jamboree,
A hoedown right in Min's saloon.
It's heel and toe, and away they go.
He's back again, Jack Rance, the goon.

"Come on," says Dick to blushing Min.
"Let's have a dance, okay?"
And although Min has never danced,
She takes Dick's hand and sways away.

That very night Dick sees the light;
He sings of love, of June, of moon;
And then and there makes up his mind,
He will not rob Minnie's saloon.

The hour is late; Min makes a date;
Invites Dick to her shack.
Dick's deep in love, can hardly wait
(And neither can Sheriff Jack).

ACT II — *Minnie's Shack*

Min starts to tidy up the joint.
She's all keyed up to make the scene.
She puts away her little gun;
Then tries to look calm and serene.

She knows a gun's a girl's best friend.
Diamonds can leave one in the lurch
In case some jerk attempts to rape
Or tries to snatch a purse.

She sticks some roses in her hair;
Then has the table set for two.
One way to get a man, 'tis said,
Is by the stomach, and it's true.

Oh, joy supreme. He's here, her dream.
He starts to clutch and steal a kiss.
She never has been kissed before,
So says, "No, no!" with emphasis.

"What a nice, cozy room," says Dick.
"Oh, do you like it?" replies Min.
"Everything in it is like you."
The furniture appeals to him.

She then goes on about her pintos
In *allegro vivace* and *lirico spinto*:
How they gallop through fields beyond the
    hills;
Then how in the mountains they go
    galloping into.

As more of this slush and gush goes on,
A storm arises, threat'ning and grim.
Thunder and lightning, hail and snow;
Not fit for a man or beast, least him.

The gentle crook says he must go.
How could he stay and compromise
This well-bred barmaid, pure as snow?
'Twould be a mistake; not very wise.

But Minnie cannot let Dick go,
So as he started to leave, she said,
"Your thoughtfulness quite touches me."
So graciously offers him her bed.

"It's madness to go out tonight;
Insane to venture out of doors.
You take my bed, I beg of you, Dick.
I've slept upon the floor before."

She begs him please to acquiesce.
"Talk through the curtains. Be my guest."
Behind the wardrobe she then goes,
Puts on her nightie with finesse.

She settles down before the grate,
Says goodnight from the floor.
The hanging curtains separate;
Virtuousness could do no more.

They settle down, sweet and discreet.
But what's this noise, this awful roar?
Loud talking, screaming oaths,
Rance and his gang burst through the door.

Crash on the scene the sheriff mean
Arrives, and with the fuzz,
He stomps and screams with words
    obscene,
Tells Min who Johnson is and was.

Right after Jack has left the shack,
Our Minnie now is mad as hell.
She lets Dick have it then and there;
And stops him when he tries to tell

Of how he got the way he is.
He blames it all upon his dad;
A desperado from a gang
Of tough *bandidos, mucho* bad.

His poor, dear ma left destitute,
Without centavos, poor, bereft;
So it was up to him—who else?—
To keep them from starving to death.

But when he met our darling Min,
He vowed from then he would go straight;
But nemesis caught up to him,
And now he fears it is too late.

She's mad, so she calls Dick a cad,
A double-dealing so-and-so.
She throws him out and slams the door;
Screams, "Don't come back, Lothario!"

Poor Min thinks she is through with him,
And as he's taking flight afright,
A shot is heard—they've got their bird.
Dick stumbles back, wounded in flight.

Desperate and sore, Minnie deplores
What's happened to her darling Dick.
She hides her wounded love upstairs;
Then slugs it out with Rance, but quick.

Rance has come back to Minnie's shack.
He sneers and jeers, "I know he's here.
I fired a shot and hit that mug."
Min laughs and says, "You're wrong, Jack
    dear."

"Cut out that 'Jack,' I'm Sheriff Rance.
I'm here on duty bound.
In case I'm wrong, I'll run along,
But swear I'll get that greaser hound!"

"Well, look around until he's found.
Go search my pad. Besides, you're mad."
"You said it, babe. It's you I crave."
He grabs and smothers her, the cad.

"I'm hot as hell, my haughty belle."
She struggles; wrenches herself free.
He chases her around the joint,
Breathes hard with sexuality.

Min grabs a bottle, which she swings,
Her cast iron virtue to defend.
And as the lecher fumes and pants,
A drop of blood falls on his hand.

It droppeth like a gentle rain,
From up above where Dick is at.
And who says mercy is not strained?
It is when dealing with a rat!

She takes a chance with Sheriff Rance.
She offers him a deal.
A game of poker will decide.
If Rance wins, Dick's fate is sealed.

So Sheriff Rance, he sees his chance
To dicker with proud Min.
I lose, you win, the deal is grim.
She sneers, "Now I'll show him."

She takes a pack right off the rack.
Two cards slip in her sock.
They start the game, and who's to blame
If she outsmarts the fox?

She cheats and wins (that's telling him).
He's lost his prey at cards.
"Get on your way," we hear her say,
"Go join your blasted avant guards."

With love and prayer and loving care,
She brings Dick back alive.
"Escape, my love," we hear her say,
"Before the pigs arrive."

But it's too late; the deviate
Is caught by Rance's gang.
This time he'll see the gallow tree;
He'll swing, he'll dance, he'll hang.

"Go say farewell to your gazelle,"
They yell, "then on your way.
You've had it, Dick, you greasy hick;
Your doom is sealed today."

He says, "I care not if I live or die.
Unloose me and I'll slit my neck.
But one last wish I beg you'll grant.
Tell Min my love is true, by heck.

Since you're bound to hurry me,
Please tell Min that I'm safe and free;
That no one did I love but she;
Then hang me on that goddamn tree!"

Here Rance jumps up, afire with ire.
He wants to punch Dick in the eye.
Those worthies hold him back by force.
Rance says, "Two minutes; then you die."

But lend an ear. What's this we hear?
It's Minnie with her colt;
Then, jumping off her horse's back,
She tells them all to bolt.

She tells these thugs, these hardboiled mugs,
"Enough, you lousy rats, enough!
Is this the way you all repay
The whiskey you got on the cuff?

"And that ain't all, you mugs who brawl,
Slug, swindle, fleece, and cheat;
I'll shoot and kill the first that moves."
She's armed up to the teeth.

They cringe and sigh, then by and by
They don't act so tough and rough.
They soon get wise; they compromise;
They're diamonds in the rough.

They cut Dick loose; take off the noose;
Give up the lynching and the strife.
Min falls into her lover's arms;
He's stuck with her for life.

"Farewell," they say. "Have a nice day."
The sleighing has been rough and hard.
Dick's glad to leave with all his parts
And miss the fate of Abelard.

They take the old Sierra trail,
Dick and our Min, so debonaire.
She's kept her virtue to the end,
When all around were losing theirs.

In baffled rage Rance slinks away.
He's mad as all get out.
Not only did he lose his prey,
He's lost the girl, the lousy lout.

CARMEN

We are now in Seville, on a wide thoroughfare,
On the left there's a guard house, at the right a long stairs.
The cigarette factory is not very far
Where girls roll cheroots and five-cent cigars.

A blonde ingenue, timid and scared,
Comes trembling, hesitant, down the long stairs,
Runs into Morales, and asks in a daze
If perhaps he might know where to find Don José.

She's told by Morales that José's on his way
To relieve the old guard, but please won't she stay?
She thanks the kind soldier but says in dismay,
"I'll return later on," then goes on her way.

Here the cigarette girls take a cigarette break;
Sing of sweet-smelling smoke as they go on the make.
With puffs, sniffs, and whiffs, they emit *la fumé*,
Blowing smoke in the eyes of the guys that might play.

It's like Spanish fly to some of those guys,
But some of the boys start rolling their eyes.
They try to act butch and sexy—*olé*;
Muy macho indeed and *también* very gay.

"Here they come," they all yell. Carmen, *la belle*,
She flies down the stairs like a bat out of hell.
Some boys crowd around, sniffing like hounds,
As Carmen seductively starts on her rounds.

She sings, "Love is a bird tameless and wild
And, like me (she sings), cannot be beguiled.
I may love tomorrow but surely not yet,
So be on your guard or you'll live to regret."

"*Quesque tu fais?*" with José she coquettes.
"I'm fixing a chain for my gun's epaulets."
She throws him a flower; then runs up the stairs.
It's the mystic acacia—bewitching. Beware!

He picks up the flower and says, "What a nerve.
Somehow it seems she's thrown me a curve.
The perfume is strange, heady, and rich.
And the girl? Who knows? She could be a witch."

Micäela returns, shyly seeking José.
She falters and wavers 'mid guards—in dismay.
She then sees José among the dragoons;
Rushes up to him frightened, ready to swoon.

She gives him a note with a few coins, and then
José sees the farmhouse, the cows, and the hens.
He'll return to the village; Micäela he'll wed;
Then looks toward the factory with a feeling of dread.

He's touched to the core; then, sighing, implores
For news of his mother, beloved and adored.
Micäela takes heart, says, timid and shy,
"She gave me a kiss to give you. Good-bye."

There's now an alarm, violent and shrill,
From the cigarette factory just over the hill.
It's a battle for fair; girls yanking at hair;
Scratching and kicking each other's derrière.

"It's Carmen," they scream. "She started the scene.
She stabbed and hit first. She's savage and mean."
Zuniga, the captain, calls Carmen "la pest,"
Has her hands tied, and prepares her arrest.

She begs Don José to help her get loose
While on the way to Seville's calaboose.
She promises thrills by the walls of Seville.
She begs him to come. She weakens his will.

As he loosens the cords, she pushes José.
He falls on his pratt. Carmen dashes away.
The collusion's exposed, reported, and then
José is arrested and thrown in the pen.

Act II – *The Tavern of Lillas Pastia*

Carmen dances and sings and plays castanets
With smugglers and soldiers that gamble and bet.
She clicks with her heels as they holler *olé*.
She's the belle of the dive where scoundrels hold sway.

Zuniga tells Carmen José's left the jug,
Has just been released, so she may see his mug.
Thereupon shouts of *viva* are heard
For the great Escamillo, the bull-slaying bird.

He vainly struts in, pompous and proud,
Proud of his fans for crying out loud.
Carmen shoots him a glance while acting blasé.
Escamillo, she knows, will be her next prey.

A voice on the way is heard; it's José,
The handsome dragoon along the pathway.
He's greeted by Carmen, contained and restrained.
She tries making him jealous with studied disdain.

She tells him she's danced for Zuniga and friends,
But she'll dance for him too, so she starts to again.
She hums as she sings and fascinates him.
Then a bugle is heard through the noise and the din.

"This is the retreat," José then explains
That he must get right back to the barracks again.
"I've danced and I've sung," Carmen says, "you dumb cluck.
And you talk of retreats. That's just my bad luck."

Here he takes from his pocket the flower she threw
And with tears in his eyes sings Sevillian blues.
"The flower you gave me went with me to jail."
He goes on quite a bit with a long-winded tale.

"I've heard that old gag," she says. "It's not true.
If you loved me the way you say that you do,
You'd desert, join my gang of smugglers, José,
Jump with me on a horse and gallop away."

A knock at the door is heard and ignored;
No matter, Zuniga comes in, and what's more
He sees Don José, tells him, "Be on your way.
You've heard the retreat. These are orders, I say."

José and Zuniga draw swords, swear, and curse.
The party gets rough; Zuniga gets worse.
The smugglers surround him and start making sport.
He gets kicked on his way, with a musket escort.

Zuniga swears vengeance as he's shoved on his way,
So the cutthroats break camp in wild disarray.
José's in a bind—won't leave Carmen behind—
So he joins the marauders; his own doom is signed.

ACT III – *A Mountain Pass*

José has deserted, escaped, left the troop.
He's now a *bandido*, a part of the group.
The inscrutable cassia indeed cast a spell.
Like the stars, it not only inclined, it compelled.

Repentant, the lug is now with the thugs—
Desperate, forlorn, and deeply in love.
But by now Carmen's love for José has grown cold.
"Go back to your mother," she sneers, cruel and bold.

Mercédès and Frasquita, with joy and with zeal,
Shuffle cards in suspense as to what they'll reveal.
"Love, wealth, and contentment," they cry in one breath.
Carmen shuffles and shuffles. Her cards predict death!

The contrabandists are forced to move on.
José's left on guard as they scurry along.
He hears someone coming; fires a gunshot.
It's Micäela; she's frightened and runs off in a trot.

José's left alone, on guard in the camp,
With orders to shoot any snooper or tramp.
When he hears someone coming, he pulls out his gat;
Shoots the brave Escamillo, right through the hat.

The shot missed his head by only a shade;
Could have ended at once his bold escapade.
He then tells José the reason he's there.
José jumps in the air, starts pulling his hair.

"Carmen?" he screams. "How dare you. She's mine.
I'll teach you a lesson, you bull-slugging swine."
Both pull *navajas*, shrieking curses and names.
They'll fight to the death for the wild gypsy dame.

Carmen, the temptress, arrives just in time,
Stops the combatants, kicks José's behind.
She then tells José to be on his way;
That she loves Escamillo, so, "Go 'way and stay."

Trembling with fear, Micäela appears.
Weeping, she cries into Don José's ear,
"Your mother is dying, keeps calling, 'José.'
Come leave these malfactors. Let's get on our way."

Between love and duty, José has no choice.
His heartstrings are wrung by Micäela's sweet voice.
To Carmen he says, "I'll go, but beware.
You'll pay through the nose. I'll be back, slut, I swear."

She sneers at José, "Get going, you flop."
Enraged, he gives Carmen a karate chop.
She sinks to the floor, screaming curses galore,
As José, on his way, screams back, "You whore!"

ACT IV - *Outside the Plaza de Toros in Seville*

We are back in Seville for the thrill of the kill.
There soon will be slaughter 'mid shouts loud and shrill.
Here are grandees, hidalgos, señoras, señors,
Dark-eyed señoritas, and gay matadors.

The crowd is ecstatic, awaiting the show.
Then they spot Escamillo, Carmen's new beau.
Carmencita is with him, dressed up fit to kill,
Anxious to cheer her lover's great skill.

Mercédès and Frasquita also are there.
Both rush up to Carmen and warn her—beware!
They tell her José is casing the spot.
Carmen couldn't care less. She'll tell him what's what.

As her ex-love appears, she sneers, "*Quel toupet.*
You know the score, Don José, so be on your way.
How many times must I tell you I'm through?
So get going, Casanova. I've had it with you."

She takes from her finger the ring that he gave;
Throws it at him with scorn, defiant and brave.
As she tries to escape, José bars her way.
"Carmen, you're damned." Then he goes on to say,

"I've pleaded, beseeched, begged, and implored
While you flaunt your new lover and act like a whore."
So saying, José warns Carmen, "Beware,"
Then reaches for his knife in grief and despair.

She sneers and she jeers and scoffs like a tart.
She defies him, so he drives the knife through her heart.
So shed no sad tears for this cold femme fatale.
It couldn't have happened to a worthier doll.

Boris Gudonov

*A*gamemnon was commander, and the first one to philander.
First he met the lovely Briseis, most complacent, willing, easy.
Klytemnestra was forgotten, which perhaps was rather rotten.
It's a fact for many years not a word did Klemy hear.
Naturally she thought him dead, as she tossed and squirmed in bed.
So one night she said, "Oh heck, I'll go to a discotheque."

There she met her husband's cousin, and he told her what was buzzin'.
This Aegisthus knew the score, handsome Greek, and what is more,
Made his mind up then and there to move in her pied-à-terre.
"Klemy dear," said sly Aegisthus, "you must not get bored and listless."
Then he told her what he'd heard of that double-dealing bird.
As one word led to another, Klemy said, "That lousy rotter."

"Me a loving wife and mother, with two most ungrateful daughters."
Looking at the handsome Greek, Klemy thought, "What a physique!"
He was more than sympathetic, sexy, strong, and quite aesthetic.
Then he said, "I must declare, you have not been treated fair.
An attractive dame like you, treated like a parvenue?
You need a man around the house," said the handsome Grecian louse.

ELEKTRA

"Please don't read the Odyssey—that's vile media," said he.
"Where there's smoke, of course, there's fire," said he to increase her ire.
Saner words were never said, so she took him home to bed.
Then together they ruled Argos, Klytemnestra and Aegisthus.
Sophocles called it adultery, which from him was rather paltry.
But who cares what's done and said, when sex rears its ugly head!

Klytemnestra as a mother was the type that makes one shudder,
Treated her two helpless daughters as no decent mother oughter.
They did all the household labor, which astounded all the neighbors.
Elektra deplored her lot, emptied pots of you-know-what!
With her mad father fixation, she was led to desperation.
The Agememnon family feud grew vindictive, bloody, lewd.

Elektra loathed Klytemnestra, cooked up evil schemes to best her;
Even told her she would die, by her own kin and blood ties.
When she vowed to kill her mother, Chrysothemis screamed and
    shuddered.
Chrysothemis, her own sister, refused flatly to assist her.
Klytemnestra, heartless mother, was a vixen like no other.
But the Fates were out to get her; she got her comeuppance later.

Orestes, her infant child, she had sent into exile.
No one knew what he became, banished by that awful dame.
Just then someone rang the bell, and Elektra said, "Oh hell."
Found an old bum standing there, with a youth below the stairs.
The old man spoke up and said, "Orestes, your brother's dead."
Elektra said, "You must be kidding, and how dare you bring such biddings?"

"Our own voodoo necromancer read tea leaves to get the answer,
Slit wide open several goats, read their entrails, gave up hope."
Then the youth spoke up and said, "I'm Orestes; I'm not dead."
"The gods be praised, dear brother mine, you arrived here just in time.
I was planning to kill mother. You can help me now, dear brother."
"Yes indeed, Elektra dear, that's the reason why I'm here."

That night while the folks were napping came a gentle tap, tap, tapping.
"Who is there," cried Klytemnestra, "waking me from my night's siesta?"
"It's only me from over the sea," said Agamemnon, filled with glee.
"How nice to be home again. Home sweet home," he said again.
Aegisthus quaked with fear and dread, ran like hell under the bed.
The Fates marched on—they're raving mad. It says so in the Iliad.

Klytemnestra said, "Doggone, why'd you stay away so long?
Let me get you some *pasticio*. Your dear cousin's dying to greet you.
Take off all that heavy armor. Welcome home," she said with furor.
Then before Agamemnon knew it, she and Aegisthus went right to it.
He was bludgeoned on the head, bled and bled, and then dropped dead.
"Now's the time," Elektra screamed. "Come, Orestes, there's the Queen!"

Suddenly, another scream. Klytemnestra's dead, it seems.
"Don't stop now, Orestes dear. Kill Aegisthus. He's right here."
So no sooner said than done, dear Orestes kills that bum.
Elektra's joy is now complete; she does a rock and roll from Crete.
Then falls senseless to the floor. Senseless? Not more than before.
The curtain falls, but that's not all. The dead come back for curtain calls.

Pelléas and Mélisande

Of all the vapid, zany blondes,
None can compare with Mélisande.
She's brooding, aimless, by a stream
Close to a fountain—off her bean.

Golaud, a hunter, dumb and strong,
Has lost his way but stumbles on.
He bumps into this flaky brat,
Who's lost but can't tell from where at!

She weeps because she's lost her crown
But won't permit to have it found.
She says, "If it's retrieved, I'll scream;
Or worse, I'll jump into the stream."

"Okay, okay," we hear him say.
"If that's your wish, have it your way;
But you can't stick around this spot;
Someone might come and—you know what."

She then agrees to follow him
Back to his castle, drear and grim.
But she's enchanted with the gloom.
She loves things doleful like a tomb.

She weds her pickup on the way.
Then, nonchalant, he stops to say,
"I'm sorry I can't take you in
'Cause dad and ma are mad as sin.

My dad is king of Allemande."
"So what? Who cares?" says Mélisande.
"Well, both my folks are snobs. Besides
They'd picked for a blue-blood bride.

I wrote a note to Pelléas;
Told him exactly how it was.
So we'll just have to wait and see
What Pelléas can do for me."

"Who's Pelléas?" said Mélisande.
"My brother, of whom I'm so fond.
Look, here comes Pelléas, the lamb
To meet the *fille aux cheveau de lin*."

Pel takes a look at Mélisande,
That evanescent, lightweight blonde.
It's surely not love at first sight;
They're both vague, like pre-Raphaelites.

But later on, down by the spring,
Mélisande's playing with her ring.
She throws it up high in the air;
It lands in the pool, way deep down there.

"What shall I say to old Golaud
When I get back to the abode?"
"Tell him the truth," says Pelléas.
"What can he do, the silly ass?"

They walk back to the castle grim,
Together—Mélisande and him.
She finds Golaud in disrepair.
His own horse kicked him, you know where.

Dear Mélisande takes care of him
With liniments and things that sting.
She wipes the blood from off his head;
Then bitter tears she starts to shed.

He gently takes her by the hand;
Then asks her, "Where's the wedding band?"
She says she lost it in a cave,
Running away from nasty waves.

"Go back and find it right away.
Take Pelléas. Do what I say.
That ring had magic powers, dumb cluck.
And if it's lost, that's your bad luck."

She sees the turret and runs upstairs;
Then suddenly lets down her hair.
Her tresses fall right to the ground,
And, boy, is Pelléas dumbfound.

His "thing" is all about long hair.
He grabs a handful then and there.
He brings the tresses to his lips,
Gets quite obscene, and almost flips.

They start more Maeterlinck-y chit,
Till Golaud gets a load of it.
Right then and there he smells a rat.
"Ye gods," says he, "it can't be that."

He grabs his brother by the neck
And takes him on a little trek.
He leads him to the dungeon's vaults.
About to push him in, he halts.

Then shortly after, hand-in-hand,
Come Pelléas and Mélisande.
He tells her that he's got to scram.
He got word from his sick old man.

Old Arkel, too, has ESP.
He seems to sense catastrophe;
Tells Mélisande, "You should have fun.
You're only young once, honey bun."

He kisses her, then goes his way;
Runs into Golaud—mad, distrait.
He's scratched his head against a tree
And carries on ferociously.

He wants no help from Mélisande.
He's had it from that dizzy blonde.
Asks for his sword and things like that;
Then grabs her hair in nothing flat.

Starts dragging her from here to there,
Not by her feet, but by her hair.
He drops her then in Arkel's lap;
Says, "She's all yours, Arkel, old chap!"

This five-act lyric drama score
Gets complicated more and more.
More characters arrive; in fact,
We have a parturition act.

Imagine Mélisande's surprise
When a tiny baby girl arrives.
"How very small she is," she sighs.
"She'll weep a lot before she dies!"

Then Mélisande starts to expire,
But Golaud cannot help inquire,
"Did you love Pelléas, my dear?"
"Yes," she says wanly. "Is he here?"

"Oh, please forgive me," Golaud said.
"For what?" she says, her senses dead.
"I know your pleasant camaraderie
With Pelléas was gay and free.

"I also know that he and you
Had several little rendezvous.
But just one thing I'd like to know,
Did you? Say simply yes or no."

She whispers no, her last bon mot.
She then expires in statu quo.
Alas, alack. In the last act,
Golaud learns Pel left Mel intact.

ACT I

I PAGLIACCI

Behold strolling players, in groups and in pairs,
Traveling on foot and muleback here and there.
Canio is chief of this mountebank troupe.
Nedda's the wife of this drip nincompoop.

Nedda is tired of the struggle and strife,
And wishes like hell she could scram from this life.
Tonio, the hunchback, a base guttersnipe,
Is deceitful and evil—a sinister type.

He's madly in love with Canio's wife.
He's bound to seduce her. He plots and connives.
Nedda is weary, disheartened, perturbed.
Sings a *ballatella*—her song's for the birds.

Tonio appears, throws himself at her feet.
Declares that he loves her, implores and entreats.
As he aims for her lips, she flees from his grip,
Then strikes the repellent freak with a whip.

In the midst of this brawl, Silvio leaps o'er the wall.
(Silvio's her boyfriend, and that isn't all.)
Nedda plans to escape with Silvio that night.
After the show, the two will take flight.

From his hiding place Tonio sees them embrace.
Rushes off to tell Canio of Nedda's disgrace.
Canio dashes and catches them both in the act.
Silvio runs for his life to avoid the attack.

"Tell me his name," screams Canio, insane.
"His name, his name," he shrieks with disdain.
The show must go on—you've heard this before.
It's an old platitude, theatrical lore.

She had faithfully promised her beau Harlequin
That she'd run away that same night with him.
Taddeo arrives with food and with wine,
Starts making advances, concealed, clandestine.

He pleads and he begs, "Oh, dear Columbine,
I beg on my knees, be mine, love, be mine."
Harlequin enters the scene just in time
To kick bold Taddeo in the behind.

Whereupon Harlequin and sly Columbine
Sit at the table, eat and drink wine.
"Tonight and forever, I am thine, Harlequin."
"Right after the show," she promises him.

Here Punchinello arrives in surprise.
It's Canio dressed in his clown-suit disguise.
"The very same words I heard," Canio cries,
"The words that she whispered to that unknown guy."

Here the plot thickens more than before.
Canio screams, "Nedda, I'm the clown nevermore.
Tell me the name of your lover," he roars,
"Deceitful, conniving, two-timing whore."

"My lips are sealed," she says. "Canio, you heel.
I've had it with you and this lousy deal."
Here Canio swoons, "Nedda, you've sealed your doom."
Then he grabs a knife, threatens, and fumes.

Canio groans and he moans. Hot tears fill his eyes.
He sobs and he cries, but he must vocalize
Ridi Pagliaccio. He bursts into song.
No matter how shattered, "the show must go on!"

He'd win an award, of that there's no doubt—
If not for *bel canto*, for crying out loud.
He wails and he weeps, as the gold curtain falls.
He keeps wiping his eyes, even through curtain calls.

AcT II

The villagers dressed in their best Sunday dress
Arrive for the show with joy and with jest.
Nedda's now dressed as the fair Columbine,
Passes the plate for nickles and dimes.

Silvio appears somewhere from the rear
And secretly whispers into Nedda's ear,
"After the show, we'll give Canio the air.
I'll be waiting, my love. Come, you-know-where."

He then takes a seat behind a tall tree,
Where he waits for her secretly, on the Q.T.
The show that goes on, strange as it seems,
Is based on deceit—the very same theme.

Fair Columbine, of course, as you know,
In the show she's two-timing Punchinello.
Deception and snare—the same as act one—
With vendetta, revenge, without paragon.

"Take that, you strumpet," Canio cries,
Then plunges the knife into Nedda, his wife.
"Silvio," cries Nedda, as she starts to die.
Silvio jumps on the stage in rage stupefied.

Silvio is stabbed by the very same knife.
Thus ends the story of vengeance and strife.
"*La commedia e finita,*" Canio cries.
"The comedy's over," he cries, mesmerized.

LUCIA *di* LAMMERMOOR

ACT I

In old Lammermoor, in the good days of yore,
The noble Scots fought and wallowed in gore.
Each other's Scotch plaids they snatched and they tore,
Clutched hand-knitted kilts, and kicked posteriors.

The Ravenswood clan and the proud Ashton kin
Were enemies, foes, through thick and through thin.
No Ravenswood dared or e'er hoped to win
A bride of Lord Ashton's sycophant kin.

Now everyone knows the old Scottish lore
Of the poor bartered bride of old Lammermoor,
Who met, by mischance, a young bachelor
Named Edgar, of Ravenswood progenitors.

'Twas love at first sight, despite feuds and war.
They pledged true devotion forever and more.
Lord Ashton found out, hit the ceiling, and swore,
Forbidding Lucia to see him once more!

But love finds a way, so the poetasters say,
And so did these lovers; they met day by day.
They met in the heather and secret pathways,
Or they kissed through the rye. Well, who is to say?

Now Norman was Lord Ashton's sly sentinel.
Whenever they met, he'd run, skip, and tell.
He scouted and spied every nook, glen, and dell,
Squealed, and made Ashton madder than hell.

The Ashtons were snobs, consumed with false pride.
Though bonny Lord Henry was scheming and snide,
He muddled and mixed on the Jacobite side
And was wanted in England for planned regicide.

Henry had (you know what) caught in the sling,
And to save it he planned nefarious things.
He'd sacrifice Lucy; sing "God save the king,"
Stopping at nothing to save his own skin.

The ready-made spouse was a wealthy old creep.
His name was Lord Bucklaw and blunt like a sheep.
No matter how Lucy did sob and did weep,
She'd fare no better than Little Bo Peep.

Lord Henry got tough, raised a hullabaloo;
Said he'd cremate Edgar, that low parvenue.
Lucy fainted away, recovered, and flew
To warn and tell Edgar what Henry would do.

As she started to talk, she felt strange in the head,
The things that she said were disconnected.
She spoke of her brother with glee and with dread.
Even Ed got confused at the things that she said.

"Now calm yourself, Lucy. Just leave it to me.
I'll go to your brother, explain, and we'll see.
Take hold of yourself. You're as shaky as can be.
I'll settle that crumb. Now listen to me.

"Please understand, Lucy. I'll make no demands.
I'll go to your brother and ask for your hand."
"My hand," cried Lucia. "I don't understand.
He might chop off both. You don't know that man."

"Oh, Lucy," cried Edgar. "You're not making sense.
If I offer marriage, he has no defense.
You see what I mean? The plan is immense.
I'll pay for the wedding, at Henry's expense."

Poor balmy Lucy, she sighed and she cried.
"My brother will scratch out your hands with his eyes.
I'm the eye of his apple," she sighed and replied,
"Who said there's two sides to a story, just lied.

Without batting an eye, he'd do sororocide.
A word to the wise is hooey," she sighed.
"By now you should know my brother's cockeyed,
So why trifle with trifles and be mortified?"

"It won't hurt to try," bonny Edgar replied.
"Why beat round the bush or the heather? Besides,
How can anyone tell? One just has to try.
I might even give him a punch in the eye."

"If at first you succeed, keep trying. Besides,
Try, try again is a silly bromide.
And he who laughs last is a silly old guy.
Better laugh first than eat humble pie."

"I do hate to mention this, Lucy, my dear,
But your whole conversation sounds loony and queer.
Go see Doc MacGregor; have a talk ear to ear.
His patients get worse, but he's very sincere."

"Oh, Edgar, my bonnie, don't be obsolete.
You know yourself, Edgar, the Doc's indiscreet.
He jumped from his window and died on his feet,
While a patient lay prone on the couch, on her seat."

"Well, I guess I'll be going," said Edgar at last.
"You have convinced me, my sweet bonnie lass.
I forget, did I mention I'm going to France?
So here are some letters I wrote in advance."

ACT II

The king summoned Henry to court to come clean,
Though Hanky would rather have dealt with a queen.
Perfidious Albion—you know what I mean?
They'd switched from a queen to a king in between.

Lord Henry was deadly in Dutch, as you know,
And Buck promised him he'd put in a bon mot.
He'd save Henry's neck, then said apropos,
"Don't forget bonnie Lucy, the old so and so."

As Lucy got vaguer, day in and day out,
Lord Henry got schemier fig'ring it out.
Lucy must marry that opulent lout.
"Like it or not," he started to shout.

The villain began with legerdemain,
With fast double talk, and catch-as-catch-can.
The letters Ed wrote never reached Lucy's hands.
She became more bewildered, could not understand.

By now bonny Lucy was torn to a shred.
Henry gave her a letter he'd forged, and it read:
"I thought that I loved you, but I found out instead
I'm in love with another, dear Lucy," signed Ed.

In a daze and half-crazed, she swooned to the floor,
Whereupon enters the conspirator.
"Dear Lucy," he sighed, "I've told you before.
Ed is a heel; wed Buck, I implore.

"Besides, Lucy dear, I am in a jam.
We're ruined completely, lest you wed this man.
I face a jail sentence; this is no sham.
Now be a good lass; sign this contract, my lamb.

"The contract's all set; the ink is still wet.
The guests have assembled in strict etiquette."
Lucy totters and shudders, signs her name with regret.
In rushes Edgar, *voilà*, the sextet.

Now here's blood and thunder, with sobs and with tears.
Vile threats, maledictions, shrieks splitting the ears.
Though they threaten each other 'mid cynical leers,
They don't move an inch, the brave cavaliers.

"Here's your ring," cries Ed, flinging a ring.
"You have shattered my faith, my very lifespring.
"And here's yours," screams Henry, as from Lucy he wrings
The gold band Ed gave her, then stomps on the thing.

They threat and rethreat, vociferous and mean.
"Let me at him," shrieks Edgar, "that Scotch Ghibelline."
While music crescendoes, they're venting their spleen.
Down comes the curtain; it's the end of the scene.

ACT III, SCENE I

The guests have assembled, all gay as can be,
Making the wedding a blithe jubilee.
They suddenly notice the two absentees
That vanished right after the "Oh, Promise Me."

"Cut out all the horseplay," we hear a voice roar.
It's Raymond, the tutor, the joy-killing bore.
Of course they stop dancing. How could they ignore
The maitre d' basso, grim, solemn, and dour?

He sings, "While eavesdropping, my ear at the door,
I heard screams and screeches and curses galore.
What was my surprise as I crashed in the door?"
"What?" sings the chorus. "The groom on the floor.

"All covered wie blood, twa surela a sight.
Wha a gift for a groom on 'is own wedding night.
Wha would gud Pastor Knox sa to see sucha fright.
A disgrace to tha church, an 'e could be right."

"Who don' it? Quick, tell us," they ask the old bass.
"'Twa the wie lassie Lucy," he says in a daze.
"Wi his own sword she killed eem," he says to their face.
"She dina e'en geeve him a wie coup de grace!"

But what's this we see? It's balmy Lucy,
Nuts as can be singing Es above Cs;
She comes down the stairs as composed as can be,
Visualizing her bonnie from over the seas.

Henry comes in, contrite, beholding the sight,
Is filled with remorse, knows he hasn't done right;
Also knows it's too late to change cruel fate.
The curtain comes down, but he's still full of hate.

SCENE 2 — *The Churchyard*

Edgar waits for Lord Henry. It's pistols for two
Or, better still, swords, which they've chosen, in lieu.
While waiting for Henry, Edgar boohoos
For the dear, dear, departed, a century or two.

He stands near a hole, mournful and dole.
As he ponders his fate, he hears a bell toll.
Some mourners drop by. He asks "Why?" and is told
That Lucia is dying, the poor, hapless soul.

They go on to tell of her forced espousal,
And why she got loony, the dear bonnie belle.
Imagine poor Edgar as they go on to tell
How her longing for him drove her pell mell.

Lord Henry, the coward, stayed home and in bed;
Forgot all about his engagement with Ed.
To that strange field of honor, he sent there instead
Old Raymond, the tutor, the old blunder head.

The toll of the bells for a soul that departs,
It's good-bye forever for Lucy, ill-starred!
"*Hout tout*, laddie boy," Raymond cries with a start,
As Ed pulls a knife, which he thrusts in his heart.

Although the blood flows, he sings from said heart,
"In heaven we'll meet, love, never to part."
He has ESP and a horoscope chart.
They'll both meet in heaven, as swift as a dart.

IL TROVATORE

Upon a day in old Biscay,
A gypsy cast a spell
On the house of Count di Luna.
And this is what befell.

They caught the hag, the gypsy bag,
And had her barbecued.
And as she turned and squirmed and burned,
These are the words she spewed.

"Go get those rats, those plutocrats.
A curse be on their heads.
Avenge me, hapless daughter. Do!"
So saying, she dropped dead.

'Mid tears and pain and half insane,
The daughter stole the child
Of Count di Luna from his crib
And rushed it to the burning pile.

ACT I

In days of yore, the troubadours
Were singing columnists.
They sang of who did what to who,
And this, one never missed.

Across the moat his song would float,
Declaiming love and passion.
He vowed he'd be forever true,
As in those days was fashion.

Leonora couldn't ask for more;
Her cup spilled o'er the brim.
She rushes to her lover's arms.
Ye, gods! It isn't him.

'Twas not the swain that wooed the dame
Accompanied by his lute.
It was the son of old di Luna,
The knave, the swine, the heel, the brute.

She tells the knight, "Go fly a kite.
You're not the one. So go away."
"I'll go, proud beauty. That's okay.
But I'll slay that crooner on my way."

The rivals meet. They swear and bleat
And pledge to cremate one another.
They lose their cool, rush off to duel,
While Leonora shudders.

At sword's point they blow the joint.
They'll settle it this time.
The count draws blood; Manrico falls
But rises on the count of nine.

Wounded, he tramps back to the camp.
His wound is almost mortal.
In Azucena's arms he drops
Within the gypsy portal.

With voodoo cures, spells, and conjures,
Together with witch hazel,
They bring 'em back alive. He vows
To slay those blue-blood *azels*.

Act II

It's now Act Two, and right on cue
You hear the anvils ringing.
And what a camp, with gypsy scamps
Singing with hammers swinging.

While anvils ring and gypsies swing,
Azucena tells a story
Of blood and lust, of fire and dust,
And vengeance, cruel and gory.

The tale's the same, about the flame,
That broiled her ill-starred mother,
And how into the pyre she threw
Her own child, not the other.

"Then who am I and who's the guy
You threw into the pile?"
"You ask such foolish questions, Man."
I simply said, "A child."

From mouth to ear Manrico hears
The dirt that has been done.
Because Le'nor's been told he's dead,
She'll take the veil, become a nun.

"A nun? A nun? How come?" He's stunned.
He rushes to the scene
Before a novice she becomes—
A lay—or Ursuline.

Almost too late, he's at the gate.
His rival got there sooner.
Fuming about, screaming, the lout,
He'll snatch her and he'll ruin 'er.

The Count di Luna, the blackguard goon,
Is close to seizing Leonor'.
But it's too late; at any rate
The rape is off. Manrico scores.

A nunnery? Catastrophe!
Imploring litanies reach the skies.
While daggers flash and swords slash,
La Macerena saves both guys.

Man says, "You dope. Only the pope
Can free you once you're in."
"I see," says she and off they flee
To live and love, just she and him.

Act III, Scene 1

For reasons unknown the gypsy roams
Into di Luna's bivouac.
She's spotted by old Ferrando;
Walks right into his cul-de-sac.

"What do you here?" the scoundrel jeers.
"I've seen your mug before, methinks."
And as she stutters, hems, and haws,
The stinker slaps her in the clink.

"Whence come you, say?" "From old Biscay.
To seek my son, the ingrate brute,
Who left me flat, imagine that,
And left me destitute."

"Who is the dame and what's *his* name?"
"Manrico. Hers is Leonor'."
"Ye gods. The rival of di Luna!"
Here the libretto thickens more.

Then in a flash, burning with rash,
He grabs the gypsy mother;
Says, "You're the dame who in the flame
Flung Count di Luna's brother."

Scene 2

Again the same castle in Spain;
The bridge, the moat where lovers met.
They pledge their love forever more.
L'amour toujour—but not quite yet.

He gets the news: savage abuse.
The gypsy's sentenced to the stake.
While Leonor' entreats, implores,
He rushes off to slay those rakes.

Act IV – *Prison Scene*

Outside the clink ready to sink,
Leonora's on the spot.
The Miserere dirge is heard.
Manrico sings, "Forget me not."

"Forget you? Me? How could that be?
How could I e'er forget your lute
Or songs you sang that used to float
Across the mout before the rout?"

"Forget me not. Forget me not."
"Don't worry," answered Leonor'.
"I'll save you, loved one, rest assured,
My one, my own, my troubadour."

And as she cries, the count stops by.
Tears and pleas he derides, ignores.
The martinet says he regrets
He can't heap on her lover more.

Again he said, "I'll see him dead,
Lest you, Leonor', become my wife."
Alas, alack. She makes a pact.
She'll fool him yet; you bet your life.

"You've won the score, noble señor.
Now let me in that prison wall."
She'll beat him still. She takes a pill.
It's arsenic, mixed with Pentothal.

Within those prison walls, she falls
Into Manrico's arms.
She begs him flee the gallow tree;
Escape from death and the gendarme.

He starts to curse, to fume, and worse.
He's mad as all get out.
"What have you done, you faithless one,
Played hanky-panky with that lousy lout?"

But Leonora starts to implore,
"Git goin' while the goin's good."
Then on the floor she sinks once more,
Just as di Luna strides in, the hood.

"What have you done, my cherished one?"
Manrico starts the floor to pace.
He picks the fainting maiden up:
It's arsenic and black lace.

She begs him fly and starts to die,
And then we hear her say,
"I'd rather die for you, my love,
Than let that blighter get his way."

"You must not die," we hear him cry.
"Come back to life and love once more."
Then in her lover's arms she swoons.
It's curtains for Leonor'.

The count, the lout, sputters and spouts.
He's been betrayed, cheated, and duped.
"Cut off his head. Bring him back dead,
That crooning, ninny nincompoop."

As this goes on we hear a song,
Like singing in a dream.
It's Azucena's voice we hear,
Recalling days placid, serene.

"We'll go away," we hear her say.
"Back to our mountain home."
And as she falls asleep, we hear
Her voice as she intones,

"Again one day you'll sing and play."
For hills and vales she's yearning.
"But wake me up if you see flames!"
The lady's not for burning.

In baffled rage back on the stage,
Di Luna rants and raves.
"He who laughs last, laughs best," he sneers.
"The head is off," he gloats, the knave.

The gypsy screams, wakes from her dream.
She trembles and she shudders.
"Laugh this one off, di Luna, you rat.
The victim was your brother!"

The curtain falls and that's not all.
The opera buffs all wonder.
What happens to Manrico's ma
After that awful blunder?

Manon Lescaut

This act takes place in old Amiens
Where *frère* and *soeur* Lescaut arrive
Upon a coach shared by a guy,
A hoary fox with youthful drive.

The brother of Manon's a heel,
Corrupt, debauched, and dissolute.
He plans to sell his flesh and blood
To a galoot, while still en route.

Returning to a nunnery
To brush up on a thing or two,
The stagecoach stops before an inn.
'Tis there she runs into Des Grieux.

Des Grieux tells students such a dame
He'd never seen, and what is more,
If Helen launched a thousand ships,
This face would launch a man-o'-war.

Lescaut, the crook, and the roué
Inside the inn discuss the fee.
It's cut and dried and bona fide;
She'll be delivered COD.

Edmondo, staunch friend of Des Grieux,
With students that frequent the inn
Has overheard the shanghai scheme,
Draws near Des Grieux, and cautions him.

The chevalier, without delay,
Accosts the charming demoiselle.
"Pray tell me, gracious maiden, do.
What is your name, I beg do tell?"

"Manon Lescaut," she sadly sighs.
"Alas, poor me, I'm on my way,
Back to the convent I must go;
My parents' wish, kind chevalier."

The chevalier without delay
Informs Manon about the plot.
She swoons, falls in his arms, and begs
For he, himself, her to abduct.

They jump into the cabriolet
That's waiting just outside the inn.
They speed away to gay Paree;
Love found a way for her and him.

As the old beau and rake Lescaut
Come to the inn, they're stupefied
To see the lovers taking flight;
The old futz's furious, contrite.

The so-and-so brother, Lescaut,
Consoles the lecher with tact,
Entreats him to rely on him,
To get Manon into his sack.

The sages say, and who'd gainsay,
That love's a many splendored thing.
But who can ignore the wolf at the door
When landlords and tradesmen knock and
    ring?

Yet poor Manon did carry on
With tea for two in a sleazy pad.
But she longed for the things that money
   can buy;
Things she'd dreamed of but never had.

So one fine day she stole away,
With crook, Lescaut, the scheming rat.
Without a word or farewell note,
She ups and leaves her lover—flat.

Jilted, abandoned, poor Des Grieux
Pulls out his hair, declares, forswears
The world, the flesh, devil-may-care.
He'll take the vows. He's through. So there!

ACT II

In eighteenth-century opulence
Manon's the old man's turtledove.
The old roué did get his way,
Which proves that money can buy love.

The creaky beau, in his own way,
Worked overtime to charm his pet.
But haute couture admiring guests
Failed to amuse the blithe coquette.

Oh, how she missed the chevalier,
Wept when she heard he'd taken the vows.
So just imagine her delight
When he arrived with sly Lescaut.

Lescaut, the double-dealing rat,
Is in the act once again; once more.
He told Des Grieux where Manon's at
And led him to her very door.

A lovers' quarrel thereon ensues;
The chevalier enraged is he,
Then once again becomes enthralled,
Falls for Manon's fiddle-de-dee.

They fall into each other's arms,
Embracing, swear *l'amour toujour*.
She'll leave the gilded cage *tout de suite*,
Though miss the luxury, for sure.

While in her lover's arms she lies,
The ancient Beau Brummel appears.
His face is red. He swears revenge.
He'll call the cops, the brigadiers.

"What graciousness, Mademoiselle.
How touching is your gratitude
Within my very walls betrayed.
What charming maiden turpitude."

"Why not, you fumbling 'ristocrat,
You creaky, creepy carapace.
Take a good look," she sneers and holds
A shining mirror to his face.

"*Merci beaucoup*, Mademoiselle,
No doubt you prefer bread to cake."
Then, bowing low in baffled rage,
Said, "*Au revoir*, Miss Rattlesnake."

Lescaut, the racketeer, the crook,
Breathless, he crashes through the door.
They've been denounced, he warns the pair,
Then rushes toward the corridor.

"Don't hesitate. Break out. Escape.
You face imprisonment, exile.
I got it from the horse's mouth
Down at the barracks. Quick. Defile."

The guards arrive and case the joint.
It's now a case of touch and go.
The flighty Manon loots armoires,
The Louis Quince and Rococo.

She makes a haul of precious gems,
Which she conceals between her cape.
She's nabbed; the gems spill to the floor;
She's blocked attempting to escape.

The broken-hearted chevalier
Will share her fate for woe or wiel.
He swears he'll follow his Manon
Who's on her way to the Bastille.

ACT III – *Le Havre*

Le Havre, the sea, the boat, a shack,
A gate, a guardhouse bleak and bare;
A barrack with projecting bars,
This is Manon's last pied-à-terre.

Lescaut points out the bribed gendarme
As he taps lightly on the bars.
A window opens; there's Manon,
As lovely as the evening star.

"You'll soon be free, my love," says he.
"Together we will flee this dump.
We've bribed that crummy racketeer,
Your brother's phony aide-de-camp."

Des Grieux is jittery just the same,
Distraught, uptight, distracted, taut.
Foreboding fears assail his mind.
He fears the deal will come to naught.

His premonitions were not wrong;
The planned escape has been betrayed.
A shot is fired. The jig is up.
Again another egg's been laid.

Meanwhile the tarts are rounded up.
The sergeant's told to call the roll:
Ninette, Ninon, Manon, Clarette,
And many others, brash and bold.

"Git goin', chicks," the sergeant says.
"Go ply your trade in southern climes,
Where men are men and freely spend.
Besides, you'll have a whooping time."

Some march along with *je m'en fiche*,
While others scoff, snort, sneer, and jeer.
Manon, in tears, sighs a farewell
To her despairing chevalier.

The chevalier pleads in dismay.
He kneels; he begs *le capitaine*
To take him on—noblesse oblige.
He says, "Okay. On board, brave man."

Oh, joy supreme; bliss unforeseen;
Togetherness, to sink or swim.
Manon resays, "Love found a way."
They're reunited, her and him.

ACT IV – *A Plain in Louisiana*

In days gone by in Louisianne,
The French dumped there their rank and file.
No boulevardiers anxious to play,
Only lascivious crocodiles.

Manon grew weary day by day,
Disheartened, cast off, woebegone.
No Vieux Carré in them there days;
Much less dinner at Antoine's.

Exhausted, fainting, worn, athirst,
Helpless they strayed through swamps and
    bogs.
No one to lend a helping hand;
No sign of life, just croaking frogs.

Manon grew feverish, worn, and spent.
She's reached the point of no return.
The heat, the bayous, gnats, and fleas;
This is the end of her sojourn.

The chevalier is torn, bereft;
Finds for Manon a place to rest
As he seeks shelter, water, help.
It's all in vain; an empty quest.

"Alone. Abandoned. Lost," she sings,
Wishing she'd not been what she's been.
She prays forgiveness for her sins;
One more repentant Magdalen.

The shadows fall. The sun has set.
Her time is up. She's on her way.
The chevalier comes back in time
Her tears and fears to soothe, allay.

Her eyes and nose are lacrimose,
A very touching, mournful scene—
A kiss—the last. He's in despair.
She dies near dear old New Orleans.

MACBETH

When Thane of Cawdor Macbeth was made, he did the Highland fling.
Then said, "A thane is not the same. I'd rather be a king!"
So on his way to dancing school, he met three ugly hags.
Said Mac, "You have a zodiac. Tell me, what's in the bag?"
"Let's see your hand," said one of them, the boldest of the three.
"Your palm reveals your destiny; a king or queen you're bound to be."
"Hot dog," said Mac, transfixed, entranced. "You girls have clairvoyance.
You've made my day. You're smart, I'll say. You really think I have a
    chance?"

"We do our best," said one with zest. "In thunder, lightning, or in rain.
Don't be a stranger. Do drop in. We're always glad to greet a thane.
We're very fond of animals, so bring some lizards, scorpions, newts;
Also some spiders, rattlesnakes, nightshade and marijuana roots.
And by the way, where were you born—the month, the year, the hour,
    the date?
Tell it the way it is, Macbeth, and we'll reveal your fate."

King Duncan was a family friend. With the Macbeths he wined and dined.
How could he know that Mrs. Mac had evil, base designs?
So one night in his Cutty Sark the Mrs. slipped a Mickey Finn.
Said, "Bottoms up, hail and good luck." Then Duncan's head began to swim.
"He's bloody swacked," said Mrs. Mac. "Let's lead him to the sack."
His guardmen creeps they'd put to sleep with pot and applejack.

"Now is your chance," said Mrs. Mac. "Go stick it in while he's in bed.
You'll never get a better chance. Go to it, Mac," she blithely said.
With this command Macbeth turned green, recalling Kipling's poetry.
"I'll tell the world the female breed is deadlier that the male," said he.
"You make me sick," said she to him, "observing the amenities.
Go on, Macbeth, I'm out of breath. Stop acting like Scotch bourgeoisie."

"Oh, come on, babe, don't be that way. I always did do what you say."
"Okay, then, here's your favorite dirk. Go right in now—wipe out that jerk!
Then splash some blood upon the cheeks of those two freaks now fast asleep.
Then holler MURDER, scream and screech, and also try your best to weep."
"Okay, dear spouse, I'll condescend, or else I'll never hear the end.
So please pipe down. I'm on my way to slay old Duncan, our best friend."

Into the spare room Macbeth went, quaking somewhat and diffident;
He plunged the dirk with one quick jerk, just like a noble blue-blood gent.
The blood splashed all over his hand and even on his gown.
"So what," exclaimed his noble spouse. "'Twas more than worth it for a crown!
And, Mac, imagine all those snobs in Edinburgh and Aberdeen,
With hate and envy they'll turn green when they hear I'm a queen."

To cover up his murderous deed, he said, "Let's give the folks a feed.
We'll serve them haggis, herring, scones, Scotch broth and homemade mead."
Macbeth himself got smashed and swacked, until he felt no pain.
Then he recalled the three old hags he'd met when he was thane.
"I'll drop in on their pied-à-terre and have my fortune told.
I'll have them read the zodiac—see what the stars foretold."
Those hags performed a boogie dance around the cauldron, rocked and rolled.
Then the old hags went into trance, and this is what they told:

"You'll not be licked till Berman Wood shall come to Dunsinane."
"Hot diggidy," replied Macbeth, "Macduff will go insane.
Trees are well-bred and dignified, and always know their place;
Not even God could make a tree leave its very own base.
I thank you, girls," he said and left. "Wait till I tell my spouse.
She'll laugh her head off and she'll say, 'Macduff's a silly louse.'"
He then recalled the prophecy the three hags once foretold;
That Banquo's son would once be king, which made his blood turn cold.

In haste he sought some hit-men thugs—arranged an ambuscade.
The hit men said, "Okay, Macbeth, but first we must be paid."
Excited and foreseeing doom, Mac paced the court from room to room,
Anxious to hear the thugs resume just how the Banquos met their doom.
Imagine how he cursed and chafed when told that Banquo's son escaped.
He tore his hair, started to swear and acted like a great great ape.

His heart and soul were filled with woe and, quite undone, feared Banquo's son
Would one fine day retaliate and do what he himself had done.
Uneasy lies the head, he found, that wears the coronet or crown,
Or Duncan's battle-ax and gown, besides his other hand-me-downs.
Macduff was really rough and tough and Macbeth's mortal foe.
Then Macduff said, "Enough's enough. It's time to stop that so and so!
Banquo was a pal of mine. We both fought side by side."
He knew not how he missed his pal until poor Banquo died.

Then in the midst of revelry Macbeth cried out, "What's this I see?
Someone is sitting in my chair. How insolent can someone be?"
Then madly screamed, "Why, it's a ghost, impudent, acting like the host.
He's standing up and seems to boast, and is about to make a toast!
Ye Gods, it's Banquo true to life. I'm going mad—where is my wife?"
What nerve, what gall, such protocol, to sit serenely in my hall!
Now poltergeists play tricks and tease, but Banquo sits there at his ease.
Is this a joke or a caprice? He's talking of his grandson Fleace."

Again he starts to tear his hair, makes threatening gestures at the chair.
Cried, "I don't care if you're a ghost. You give me *mal-de-mer*.
He screamed and screamed oath after oath, completely lost his cool.
"Be on your way, you stubborn mule, you ghoul, you molecule!"
Though Lady Macbeth kept her cool, Macbeth kept acting like a fool.
She told some guests, "He's sick, I think. He should be going to a shrink."
The guests all scattered, fled and flew, as pandemonium grew and grew.
The thanes and thanesses fled, too. Lady Macbeth said, "He's cuckoo!"

Then Lady Macbeth cracked up too, got looney-wacky in the head.
She can't get Duncan off her mind, nor how the old duck bled and bled.
She walks wide-eyed and stupefied, and creeps along the stairs;
"Out damn spot, out!" asleep she cries, frightened and in despair.
She's tried soaps and detergents advised on her T.V.
But though she's washed and washed her hands, she's found no recipe.
Cross-eyed she creeps from side to side, asleep but open-eyed.
Some said she fell and broke her neck; others said it was suicide.

When Macbeth heard that men at arms were out to get his arse,
He rounded up a crummy crew, diminutive and sparse.
At Dunsinane, growing insane, he waited for the foe.
But when he saw the forest move, he got the vertigo.
You can't imagine his surprise, to see the trees acting humanized.
Some marched as Scotch broom, poison oak, green shrubs and otherwise.
Macbeth said, "This is quite obscene. How dare trees act like human beings?"
Then suddenly he realized they weren't trees, but men disguised.

Macduff screamed, "Ho, you regicide, you and your cockeyed bride.
You plumb forgot that there was Fleace, Banquo's grandson, you homicide!"
Macbeth turned white and grabbed his axe, trembling with fear and dread.
Macduff beat Macbeth to the punch, and with his sword sliced off his head.
He gave the head to Malcolm, a relative of Duncan's clan.
"It's much more blessed to take than give, so take this head, young man."
Malcolm became the Scottish king and ruled the hard-boiled Scots.
His clan begot Queen Mary, whose queenly lot was not so hot.

Un Ballo in Maschera

"Thou shalt not covet thy neighbor's wife"
Is a commandment, and it could be right.
Rhinhart's conscientious and very well-bred,
Keeps books even when with his wife he's in bed.
Amelia's in love with Sir Richard, too.
She's very perturbed, can't decide what to do.
Also the Rhinharts are blessed with a child,
So one's domicile must not be defiled.

At a gathering one night in the Governor's Hall
Rhinhart, the computer, dashes in like a squall.
He rushes to Dick, breathless tells of a plan
To assassinate him, implores him to scram.
At this social bash, some witch-hunters crash,
Leading a black girl bewildered, abashed.
"I am no witch," the captured girl cries,
"These people are lying, they're nothing but lies."

Richard laughs in their face, liberates her with grace;
Then, for a lark, plans to visit her place.
Samuel and Tom are two murderous thugs,
Like Laurel and Hardy, supercilious mugs.
Of course without bassos, no opera's complete,
So the bores come and go, but are quite obsolete.
They're always together, connive and contrive,
That that night they'll take Sir Dick for a ride.

Here the plot thickens, as opera plots do.
Richard arrives at the seers' rendezvous.
Seems Ulrica's drawing an S.R.O. crowd,
Has her palm crossed with gold, for crying out loud.
In her cauldron she stirs magic voodoos,
Tells the past and the future, as she barbecues.
The seer is not fooled by the seafaring guy.
It's simple to see, it's Dick in disguise.

"You'll be killed by the guy that next shakes your hand."
"Not really," laughs Richard, skeptical, bland.
He then tries to shake hands with the conspirators,
But the bandits withdraw from the good governor.
The two crooks guffaw, pretend it's a joke.
They're saved by Rhinhart, the bookkeeping bloke.
Old faithful Rhinhart again reappears,
To warn Dick once more that the bandits are here.

He shakes hands with Dick, but just wait and see,
The sorceress was right, the killer is he.
Amelia arrives at the barbecue scene,
As Dick hides himself where he cannot be seen.
Ulrica chases the rest out at once,
So Amelia can have a private seance.
She confesses in tears of her illicit love,
Begs the witch for an anti-love potion, poor dove.

ACT II – *The Gallows Field*

The witch told her she must make rituals and rites
At a desolate hanging ground, late in the night.
She must dig up some roots at the foot of the grave,
Make a potion and drink it and she will be saved!
Amelia obeys, though in fear and in fright,
Goes to the burial place late in the night.
As she's digging away, guess who comes strolling by?
Sir Richard of Warwick—and is she surprised!

She's quite mystified. Well, wouldn't you be?
To run into Dick by the old gallows tree?
She confesses she loves him with tears in her eyes.
Sir Dick understands. He's a regular guy.
Strange as it seems, Rhinhart's back on the scene
Again to warn Warwick of the murderer's scheme.
He says, "Skip along, sir, there's no time to lose.
Get going," he says, "or you're a dead goose."

After warning Dick to run for his life,
Rhinhart sees the strange dame, doesn't know it's his wife.
How could he tell with a veil on her face?
Especially at night in this dark, gloomy place.
Richard explains that she's gathering herbs
For her old English garden, or something absurd.
Richard begs Rhinhart before he departs
To be the mysterious dame's bodyguard.

He must promise he'll not try to know who she is.
"Just walk her to town, Rhin. Promise me this."
Read on, music lover, the rest of this plot.
I'm not making this up, believe it or not.
How could Rhinhart guess or even surmise
That this is his wife with a veil for disguise.
Richard makes his escape, gets away just in time,
Just as the two creeps arrive for the crime.

The two knuckleheads discover instead
That it's Rhinhart, and Richard their victim has fled.
In their fury they tear off Amelia's veil.
Rhinhart's astounded, looks as though he's impaled.
"How shocking, Amelia. It's hard to believe
That you played hanky panky, betrayed and deceived."
Amelia pleads innocence. She cries and she moans.
Rhinhart says, "Strumpet—thumb your way home."

ACT III – *Room in Rhinhart's Home*

Rhinhart is pacing the floor, quite perturbed,
When a knock at the door is suddenly heard.
It's Amelia, repentant. She tries to explain.
Rhinhart is adamant. She's tarnished his name.
He's very upset, between me and you,
Tells her he's through, then he sings *Eri tu*.
He's planning to slay her. He can't let her live.
He simply cannot forget and forgive.

She begs on her knees her baby to see.
"Never," says Rhinhart, in cold irony.
He then changes his mind—tells her it's okay.
"Embrace him but once, then be on your way."
Oscar the page arrives on the scene.
She's a coloratura, sings high C's, D's, and E's.
She gargles cadenzas, staccatos, and all,
Then invites one and all to the governor's ball.

Amelia warns Dick in a secretive note
That the thugs are en route to kill, slit his throat.
The page spills the beans, tells how Richard is dressed,
So at the masked ball he's stabbed in the chest.
"I've had it," says Rhinhart, "you deceiving rat.
Take that, and that, and that and that."
"I'm dying," gasps Richard, "but before I go
I swear that Amelia is as pure as the snow.

"I've never touched her, not even one hair.
She's innocent, Rhinhart. I swear it, so there."
These are the last words that Sir Richard said.
Rhinhart's dumbfounded, and is his face red.
To Amelia what happens is not very clear.
After the ball she's left standing there.
'Twas Antonio Somma that cooked up this mess.
Dead these many years, he couldn't care less.

Herod, Tetrarch of Judea, is a dissolute pariah.
He usurped his brother's throne, with the aid of Herodias.
Those two murdered Herod's brother, then they wedded one another.
It was not a happy marriage, but no worse than is the average.
Herodias, Salomé's mother, is a vile bawd of the gutter,
And was known throughout the nation for her moral deviations.
And, in fact, like Hamlet's mother, she too had her husband smothered.
History says she was a slut, without ifs, or ands, or buts.

Salomé, she is her daughter, psychopathic like her mother.
But not as bad as she is painted by those guys who smeared and tainted
Salomé, wanton, obscene, though she's only in her teens.
She should be pitied and not censured for her necrophile adventure.

But to go on with the story that's incestuous and gory,
John the Baptist, the Levite, yells and screams with all his might.
He hurls threats, abominations, at the Herods, at the nation.
With his matted hair and beard, paranoic, strange and weird,
He eats locusts and wild honey, keeps his weight down but looks scrawny.
More about this zealot later, Jokanaan, the woman-hater.
Narraboth, the Syrian guard, is a docile Saint Bernard.
He is moonstruck, more or less; so are all the balmy rest.

SALOMÉ

Salomé comes on the terrace, says the banquet room is airless.
She's fed up with all those brawls, squabbling Jews, Romans, and all.
Narraboth, the Syrian guard, can't control his bleeding heart;
Though he is a hunk of man, Salomé gives not a damn.
She hears Jokanaan blaspheming. "Whore of Babylon," he is screaming.
"Strumpet, bitch, adulteress, whore—cursed are your progenitors!"
"He is speaking of my mother," said Salomé. "There is no other!
Her strange moral deviations have made Mamma more than famous."

"Don't look down at me," John cries, "with those lustful painted eyes."
"It's your hair I'm mad about!" She says, "Let me kiss your mouth."
"Evil came into the world by a woman," Jokan' scolds.
"'Bout that apple?" said Salomé. "That's baloney and a phony."
Then she said, "Your flesh is cold. I'd not touch it with a pole.
Like Medusa's is your hair, twined with snakes and asps—so there!
Let him out, guard, I demand!" Said Salomé, "I command!"
Narraboth could not resist her, so he opened up the cistern.

Then he stabbed himself and died. No one worried. No one cried.
From the cistern out he comes, skinny, bony Jokanaan.
"Touch me not!" he yells and screams. "Whore of Babylon, unclean!"
Salomé, wanton at heart, dissects Jokanaan apart.
Thinks he's chaste. Oh, what a waste. She'll seduce him and in haste.
"Suffer me to kiss your mouth. Come on, John, be a good scout!"
"Slut of Sodom, get away. Touch me not!" we hear him say.
Thereupon he leaves her cold, crawls back into his black hole.

The court enters then and there. Herod's drunk, staggers, and swears.
"Where is Salomé?" he asks. "Left the banquet—where's she at?"
"She's right there," said Herodias. "Drunken ass, can't you see her?"
"Salomé, come drink with me. I am sad. Please dance for me."
Again Jokanaan is heard, hurling curses, nasty words.
"There she is," screamed Jokanaan, "evil whore of Babylon."
"Hand him over to the Jews," said Herodias, the shrew.
"Hand him over," the Jews squeal. "We'll get rid of that *schlemiel*."

"Herod's bound Salomé'll dance. He's determined. He's entranced.
He'll give her whate'er she seeks—gems, peacocks with painted feets,
Half his kingdom—what a chance. What a deal for just a dance."
"Half your kingdom, you big louse!" screamed Herodias at her spouse.
"Do you swear it, Tetriarch?" Salomé asked the oligarch.
"Okay, Herod, that's an oath. I will dance without my clothes.

"I'll dance first with seven veils, just for biblical detail."
"Wonderful, my darling child," answered Herod with a smile.
Salomé started to dance motionless as in a trance.
The dance grew frantic, weird and wild, till she crumpled in a pile.
When she finished she was nude, in a shameful attitude.

Red-hot Herod blew a fuse, panted hard, amused and lewd.
"Come to me," he drooled with glee, "come my sweet and get your fee."
Salomé stepped close and said, "The head of Jokanaan, the head!"
"Atta girl," Herodias said, "Salomé's a thoroughbred."
Herod begged her to recant. Salomé was adamant.
"The head of Jokanaan," she screamed. "You swore it, Herod. Don't
be mean."
He tore his hair. He begged and pled. Salomé screeched, "The head,
the head!"

Defeated, angry, going mad, he'd made the oath—'twas iron clad.
Must be fulfilled, alas, alack. She won the necrophiliac.
When Herod saw the head he frowned. Said, "Now 'twill be all over town.
And if it gets to Rome and Caesar, no doubt he'll have one of his seizures.
He's temperamental, apropos. Rome whispers it *pianissimo*.
Then when he saw what Sally did with John the Baptist's severed head,
He blew his top. He cursed and swore. Said to his soldiers, "Kill that whore!"
They crushed Salomé 'neath their shields. No girl deserved a better deal.

In Venice one day by the old Grand Canal,
In a stately palazzo that looked to the sea,
The fair Desdemona lived life a devotee
With her senator dad, a Venetian grandee.

But sooner or late', no doubt it was fate,
A black man of mettle appeared on the scene.
His name was Otello and I'm here to tell you
He had what it takes, if you know what I mean.

Desdemona's dad was delighted and glad
To listen to stories Otello would tell;
And the blonde Desdemona, a Venetian madonna,
Was there omnipresent, an eager gazelle.

Though she acted sedate, she was anxious to date
The black man with courage and something innate!
She counted the days, the hours, and ways
When Otello and she could indeed integrate.

Not only the stories enchanted the houri.
She fell deep in love with the brave blackamoor.
So one day she fled and was secretly wed,
Unknown to her father, the choleric fathead.

OTELLO

When Brabantio, her dad, found it out, was he mad!
He never expected they'd do such a thing.
He fumed and he cursed Otello and, worse,
Brought Otello to court, started raising a stink.

The senate in Venice got bored with the menace;
The Turks were in Cyprus creating a mess.
So they dismissed the case against the black ace
And sent him to Cyprus to fight. SOS!

Connubial bliss both was hers and was his.
The two colors blended unblemished, and how;
So as he went to war, he asked a signor
To amuse Desdemona, then lifted a brow.

His name was Mike Cassio; he had *braggadocio*.
He was gay and serene, like a true Florentine.
"A lady's companion," sneered Iago, the fiend.
"Indeed she'll be safe with that gay Ghibelline!"

Then a friend he became to the Venetian dame,
Platonic as Plato, if you know what I mean.
But more of this later and, too, of the baiter,
Iago, the scoundrel, the villain supreme.

ACT I – *Cyprus. The Fifteenth Century.*

Iago, the fiend, was inhuman and mean,
A villian, a knave, a rogue, and a cheat.
He could make vermicelli out of Nick Machiavelli,
His Italian fine hand was finer complete.

Cassio he hated and abominated
'Cause Otello raised Cassion to a higher degree.
So with cunning deceit, he planned Cassio's defeat,
Got him drunk as a skunk, and chortled with glee.

He cooked up a plot involving the sot,
A duel with Montano, the stooge of the lot.
They fought and they spat in groggy combat,
Rang the bells of alarm, and other such rot.

The Moor had dispelled the Turk infidels,
Yet the mob rose in riot and acted like hell.
'Twas then that Otello jumped out of bed
With his bride at his side, Desdemona, *la belle*.

On going back to bed to Cassio he said,
"I cancel your rank, you blankety-blank.
You're drunk and what's more you created this roar.
Get out of my sight, you cheap mountebank!"

ACT II – *Hall of the Palace*

A fiend couldn't dream a more sinister scheme,
But Iago well knew what jealousy'd do.
So with intrigue unknown three birds with a stone
He'd kill and destroy with Italian voodoo.

To his wife he then said, "Look here, knucklehead.
I want you to get me a kerchief, you hear?
Not for blowing my nose, I've plenty of those,
But this one I ask for is special," he sneered.

"It's the one that the Moor gave his high-born amour.
I love the design for reasons of mine.
I'll have the thing copied and return it, my dear.
Don't forget, it's the one with the berry design."

Then the snake in the grass that none could surpass
Went to Cassio with fraud and phony regret;
Said, "Go see Desdemona, the incarnate madonna.
Explain what has happened. She'll help you, I bet."

Cassio took his advice, need not be told twice;
Begged the fair Desdemona to intercede, please!
She, of course, gave him tea and much sympathy,
And promised she'd help in his hour of need.

She then went to her spouse, told how Cassio got soused,
"And that's why he did what he did," she explained.
"And now he's chagrined and hopes to rewin
The office he lost because drink was to blame."

Full well Iago knew Otello's IQ;
Though a hero in war, in peace he was slow.
But Iago's fine hand needed no IBM
For calculating his nefarious blow.

"I like not that," said Iago, the rat,
As Cassio was leaving the Moor's habitat.
He then dropped a hint, or perhaps even two,
In the ear of Otello, and so that was that.

"One's peace of mind should not be undermined
By questioning the virtues of ladies so chaste,
Like your own charming consort and trustworthy wife.
'Twould be a pity indeed," said he, sly, double-faced.

Already a doubt was spread by the lout,
And sooner or later it would percolate
In the mind of the Moor, slowly, but sure,
Although Iago, the snake, begged Otello have faith.

"I know," said Otello to the vile, scheming fellow,
"My wife loves feasting, dancing, and fun,
But where virtue's concerned she's indeed very stern,
And one must have proof before evil is done."

Iago suggested that he wait and just see
How much pressure she'd use in Cassio's behalf.
"'Twould be a good sign should she act clandestine,
But, of course, one mentions this thing for a laugh."

The Moor grabbed his throat and swore he'd garrote
Any friend that would falsely his wife inculpate.
"If a man steals my purse, that's trash, as you said.
So better think twice before it's too late."

'Twas then Iago said, indignant and red,
"How could you e'er doubt my integrity?"
He then said with grace, "Cassio did wipe his face
With a kerchief embroidered with red strawberries."

The Moor in despair said, "I do declare
That is the kerchief I gave to my wife.
A curse on their heads. I'll see them both dead!"
Then he rushed from the room in horror and strife.

Desdemona said, "Hi," as she greeted her guy.
"So what about Cassio?" the poor dumb cluck said.
Otello went grim, jumped out of his skin,
Almost turned white, went out of his head.

Said he, "Desdemona. I don't like the aroma.
Are you or are you not faithful to me?"
"Why, my noble lord," she said, somewhat bored,
"Why not show Cassio your kind clemency?"

He called her a whore, threw her down on the floor,
Demanded she show him the hanky, then said,
"The thing is bewitched and woe to the bitch
Who lost it or made hanky-panky in bed."

She was clean out of luck, the poor blonde dumb cluck,
And it dawned on her then what Otello had said,
So instead of defending herself as she should,
She simply decided to go home and to bed.

Like Little Bo Peep, she started counting her sheep
And fell fast asleep, as strange as it seems.
Then Otello dropped in, armed to the teeth,
Kissed her twice on the brow, as she woke from her dreams.

He was madder'n hell, called her a Jezebel,
Asked for the hanky, again and again;
Not for blowing his nose, as everyone knows,
But to make something of it. She then knew 'twas the end.

She tried to explain, again and again,
But the half-crazed Otello had made up his mind.
For her sin she must pay; there was no other way.
She must pay for her crime and must die in her prime.

So with no more to do, the poor ingenue
Was strangled and smothered, right in their bed.
Then, ah, cruel fate, too, too much, too late,
The truth was discovered, and was his face red?

Yes, murder will out, of this there's no doubt.
'Twas Emilia that roared as she dashed through the door.
She had found Desdemona breathing her last,
Smothered to death by Otello, the Moor.

"Come one and all," she shrieked through the hall.
"Otello has murdered my mistress, his bride."
With that she indicted, incited the Moor,
Though he tried to defend his foul homicide.

In bed all alone, Desdemona did moan.
"I die guiltless and faultless," she dyingly said.
Then everyone cried as she started to die,
And all just because the Moor was misled.

The handkerchief deal, Emilia revealed,
As one and all shuddered, holding their breath.
Here Iago, the rake, the scoundrel, the snake,
Stabbed the faithful Emilia, his wife, unto death.

Otello then said, "I sure made a mistake,
But the things I did hear did discombobulate.
So when you these unlucky deeds do relate,
Just say I loved wisely, don't extenuate."

So saying, he reached for his sword and he said,
"Without Desdemona I'd rather be dead."
He staggered and swooned in fear and in dread,
Plunged his sword in his heart, and fell over the bed.

Then Iago, the rake, made a dash to escape.
He was caught by the crew, restrained, and subdued.
This story, 'tis said, is historic and true,
Which just goes to show what a hanky can do.

Act I

La Gioconda

*L*a Gioconda's quite a gal, hangs around the Grand Canal.

She sings ballads and Stornelli, also arias from Ponchielli.

She's not dressed like ordinary, singing minstrels—quite contrary.

She goes in for *haute couture,* silks and satins, to be sure.

Though the Venice streets are dirty, she wears trains. Says, "I should worry."

And her songs are sure to gather sailors, tourists, and regalers.

All the tourists stop to hear her. One and all throw coins and lire.

She is tall and real dramatic, double-breasted, operatic.

Strange enough as it may seem, she's in love with a Marine.

He's a noble Genovese, *tenor spinto*, sings high C's.

Gioconda supports her mother, who is blind, completely, utter.

Though she's friends with this Marine, La Gioconda's not his dream.

Enzo is his given name, and he loves a high-born dame.

But she's in a strange position. Her spouse heads the Inquisition.

She would stray the narrow path, but she fears her husband's wrath.

Caesar Borgia next to him is a sainted seraphim.

But about this scoundrel later, him and Barnaba, the baiter.

La Gioconda's ma, La Cieca, sings contralto discs for Decca.

But to go on with this story that is rather dull and boring,

She tries hard to vamp and snag, but she's really not his bag.

Just the same, Gioconda's game. Bound to get him, silly dame.

But vile Barnaba, the spy, says he'll get Giocond' or die.

Yet, Gioconda slips away every time he makes a play.

Hot or cold, he's bound to get her, so he's planning a vendetta.

He will take it out on mother, whom he plans to drown and smother.

He swears that the poor blind lady is a witch, mystic and shady;

That she's cast an evil spell on a seadog's Caravelle.

It's the boat of tough Zuane, who attacks the poor blind dame.

She's saved in the nick of time by dear Laura from this crime.

So she gives her rosary to Laura, who has set her free.

"Take this rosary," says she. "It will bring you luck, you'll see."

And it does, matter of fact, but that's in the second act.

Worser than a woman spurned, he is back—Barney, the worm.

He'll kill two birds with one stone. He's a Helden baritone.

First he has Isepo write to Alvise, late that night.

His beloved wife will be with her lover, out at sea.

Alvise is mad as hell, tears his beard and hair as well.
If it's true, Laura must die. He'll not have a battered bride.
Since she's left out in the lurch, poor Gioconda goes to church.
Where else can the poor girl go, spurned by Enzo Grimaldo?
Despite all this melodrama, all the cast dance La Furlana.
Joy and rapture, gladness, glamour—everybody goes bananas!

ACT II – *The Lagoon*

Barnaba is now disguised as a sailor; none get wise.
This is operatic lore. Accept nonsense and ignore
An apparent dumb disguise any fool would recognize.
Just then our hero arrives. Everybody greets the guy.
Enzo looks up at the sky, clears his throat to vocalize.
Then he sings *Cielo e Mar* to the sea and to the stars.

But the Fates, always bizarre, can't care less about the stars.
They've cooked up a dirty scheme to destroy Enzo's fair dream.
La Giocond' and Laura's there. Now they slug it out for fair.
The soprano and the mezzo start their own strange intermezzo.
Laura sings, "He is my life!" La Gioconda pulls a knife.
Laura's saved! Gioconda sees her dear mother's rosary.

Not even Euripides, Ellery Queen or Sophocles could imagine scenes
    like these.
But Boito and Ponchielli can give school to Machiavelli!
Laura's saved 'mid tears and fears, just as Alvise appears.
He is thwarted then and there by Gioconda's *savoir faire*.
She helps Laura to escape, thus avoiding the mad ape.
Then, in spite of Enzo's scorn, she alerts him and she warns

That the galleys are en route, to pursue and persecute.
Enzo, now in mad despair, curses, swears, and tears his hair.
Sets his ships afire—so there! He defeats their well-laid snare.
Here's incendiary drama, on Venetian panorama.
The pirates all arrive too late. Enzo keeps another date.
Then the curtain falls at last, on this blazing, smoking blast.

ACT III – *Hall in the Palace of Alvise*

The plot thickens, gets perverse. Ag'tha Christie at her worst.
'Cause Alvise's pride is hurt, Laura'll die. She's being coerced.
He's aghast with rage enflamed. Laura's ruined his family name.
Then and there he calls his wife, tells her she must take her life.
Handing her a poison vial, says, sardonic, with a smile,
"You will take this and you'll die, double-crossing Lorelei."

Here Boito and Ponchielli again outdo Machiavelli.
"Let's make Laura cataleptic, mix some drugs with antiseptics.
We will have her die dejected, then we'll have her resurrected."
"How'll we get Gioconda there?" Said Ponchielli, "That takes dare."
"With a mask and a falsetto, looking like a Canaletto.
She can crash the goddamn ball, hide behind one of the walls."

"That's a lulu," said Ponchielli, "just the thing, right up our alley!"
Then, without a pang of fear, La Gioconda reappears.
With sleight of hand and guile, takes the lethal poison vial.
Switches it with sleeping pills that will make her sleep until—
Wait awhile and you will see a most strange catalepsy.
Then Gioconda slips away. Once again, she saves the day.

Here Alvise enters, smiles, and beholds the empty vial.
"She has paid for her deceit," he says, chortling with conceit.
Then within the Ducal halls, he receives guests for the ball.
If Miss Maxwell were alive, even she could not contrive
Such a strange *charivari* as you are about to see.
For to while the hours away, he's arranged a dull ballet.

Here the Houris dance and sway, *entre-chats* and *tour jetés,*
Pirouettes, leaps and pliés, *pas de chats* with *toujours* gay.
"How time flies," the sages say. Not in this dreary ballet!
Guests arrive in bright attire, ready for the *Grand Soirée.*
Alvise is on the scene, greeting guests with gracious mien.
Meanwhile, Barnaba with cheer, whispers into Enzo's ear

That his lovey-dove is dead. Enzo goes out of his head.
He unmasks, pulls out a knife, ready for another strife.
Once again, the double-take, Enzo calls the duke a snake.
"It was you who stole my bride!" Enzo screams, amortalized.
Who was it who stole whose bride (quite a puzzle to decide)?
True that Laura was betrothed, to Enzo. so we're told.

But Alvise, one fine day, married her and ran away.
So the public must decide who it was who stole whose bride.
Here the duke parts the portiers, and reveals a funeral bier.
All the revelers yell and scream at this mortuary scene.
Laura lies flat on a plank, looks quite dead, with candle banked.
Enzo then with his poignard tries to murder the *canard.*
But he's seized by the duke's men, who drag Enzo to the pen.

ACT IV – *A Ruined Palace on the Guideca Island*

Since Gioconda can't find mother, she decides there is no other
Way to end her tragic life, but to commit suicide.
She's helped Enzo out of prison, so she starts her *Kyrie Eleison.*
Enzo calls her a hyena, epithets dirty and meaner.
"You've deprived me of my love!" Then he starts to push and shove.
It's another double-take. He insults her by mistake!

He swears on the crucifix that she helped him in his fix.
"I removed her from her tomb, and released her from her doom."
Enzo thinks Gioconda lied, so attacks her with his knife.
Just then Enzo hears a cry, "Enzo, dear, I'm still alive!"
Laura comes forth. They embrace. Joy supreme again takes place.
Laura tells him of her strife. La Gioconda saved her life.

Enzo falls upon his knees, then he starts to anti-freeze.
Calls Gioconda "lamb of God," noble creature—that's not odd?
I've explained the reason why, so don't be angry at the guy.
She then helps them on their way, but what a price she's had to pay:
Barnaba has named the price—she herself, what sacrifice!
Just as Barnaba arrives, he hears La Gioconda cry,

"I have kept my word," she said. "I've not lied, nor have I fled.
Take me, demon. I'm all yours!" Stabs herself, falls to the floor.
Then the rat screams in her ear, "I have drowned your mother, hear!"
But Gioconda's dead and gone, and the curtain falls forlorn.
It's a script one can't forget, a true singing *Police Gazette.*

The Flying Dutchman

La Forza del Destino

ACT I — *In the Castle of the Marquis of Calatrava near Seville*

In the first act, not based on fact,
We hear the Marquis say good night
To Leonore, whom he adores,
His loving child, his heart's delight.
While on his way to bed he says,
"I'm happy, Leonore, that
You gave the gate, before too late,
To that half-breed Inca rat."

But sex is many a wondrous thing,
Despite the ties that bind,
And Leonore plans to elope,
Leave home, Papa and all, behind.
The Señorita fell in love
With this *muchacho* from Peru,
But the Marquis is adamant;
To him all Incas are taboo.

The half-breed Inca from Peru
Jumps from the balcony on cue.
The two embrace. "Let's blow the place,"
So says the Inca parvenue.
"Seducer brash, I'll cook your hash;
You'll die," says the enraged Marquis,
While Leonore starts to implore
Her dad in tears and bended knees.

"Your daughter, noble sire," says he,
"Is just as pure as was Marie.
"'Tis I alone who am to blame,
Unheeding the amenities.
So take my life if you desire,
And let me at your feet expire."
The pistol he threw on the floor—
Went off, and killed the noble sire.

Before he died, the noble sire
Cursed Leonore with smoldering ire.
"My curse's on your head," he said,
Gave up the ghost and then expired.
Leonore with the Inca flee.
Both get lost in this potpourri.
They never meet again, you'll see,
Until the last act agony.

ACT II, SCENE 1 — *The Kitchen of the Inn in Hornacuelos*

This scene is full of noise and cheer,
Peasants and smelly muleteers;
And sure enough Don Carlo's there,
Seeking the killer, debonair.
Carlito wasn't home the night
His dad was killed and Sis took flight;
But ever since that fatal night,
He's sworn he'll kill the two on sight.

Coincidence, as you will see,
Again starts working mysteries.
Leonore, too, comes to the inn;
Imagine, runs right into him!
Although they both meet vis-à-vis,
He does not recognize it's she.
She's dressed in men's clothes—bourgeoisie—
To hide her own identity.

And now some pressure's brought to bear;
The phony student must declare
Just who he is and where he's from,
His calling and his *nom de guerre*.
He tells the Mayor he's on the scent
Of an assassin and hell-bent
To find the murderer who killed
The father of his dearest friend.

SCENE 2 – *At the Convent Gate at Hornacuelos*

"At last I'm here," said Leonore,
Just as she reached the convent gate;
In trembling fear she pulls the cord
That rings the bell above the grate.
In fright and fear she hears the sound
Of old feet scraping on the ground.
Father Guardiano then appears
And asks in basso tones profound,

"Who are you, sir? What seek you here?
Speak up, don't be afraid."
He learns it is the Vargas girl,
Dressed as a man in masquerade.
In deep distress, she tells the rest,
Her father's curse, her fright and fear.
The old monk listens, more or less,
And even tries to shed a tear.

"You've sure got spunk," says the good monk,
"So you may stick around.
We've got a cave, once occupied,
Within these holy, sacred grounds.
In a monk's robe, 'mid rocks and coves,
You can pray there both day and night.
I'll send a loaf of bread at times,
And water, too. Bless you; sit tight."

ACT III – *A Military Camp Somewhere in Italy*

And talk about coincidence,
The stars, and fate, and destiny,
Alvaro and Don Carlo are
In the same camp in Italy.
How both got there incognito
Is neither here nor there;
In opera, as in love and war,
Absurdity is more than fair.

Another bit of happenstance,
Believe it if you will or can,
Carlo gets mixed up in a brawl
With cutthroats from a robber gang.
He screams for help as he's attacked,
About to lose his life,
Cheated at cards, by scum at large,
With *navajas* and knives.

He's saved just in the nick of time
From murderers that flee.
Alvaro brings him back alive.
For crying out loud—that's destiny!
"How can a guy of noble birth,
A fact that's plain to see,
Get mixed up with those lousy hoods?"
Alvaro says, "Enlighten me."

They both tell lies and try to hide
Their true identity;
Give *noms de guerre,* then vow and swear
Eternal fealty.
Then hand in hand the *bonne camarades*
Rush off to win the war;
Fight side by side, with Spanish pride,
Like latter-day conquistadors.

Alvaro's wounded in the chest,
Fighting in war in Italy.
Both he and Carlo, side by side,
It's fate or else astrology.
Alvaro prays that he will die;
He's had it, so hopes it's the end.
Don Carlo gives him loving care—
A friend in need indeed's a friend.

Alvaro hands Carlo a case,
Before they start the great duet
Of pledges, word-of-honor vows,
'Mid blood and tears and sweat.
The great Hidalgo swears and vows
By all that's holy, he'll be true.
If Al should die, he'll burn the case.
Alvaro says, *Merci beaucoup.*

Carlo, like the great aristocrat,
Still believes in tit for tat.
Not to defend one's honor's like—
The same as straining at a gnat.
And though his conscience bothers him,
He's planning to untie the string;
Besides, he'll only take a peek;
Then burn the case and all the things.

He has another qualm or two,
Then he breaks through Alvaro's case.
A portrait falls upon the ground—
"Mio Dios," it's Leonore's face.
"It's he," he screams, "that S.O.B.;
At last I've got that rat.
I'll murder him, that's what I'll do,"
So spake the great aristocrat.

Just then the surgeon of the camp
Says joyfully, "Your friend will live."
"But not for long, I'll swear to that,
That half-breed Inca fugitive."
Alvaro rushes through the door,
Starts to embrace the grand señor.
"I'm well again, my faithful friend,
And even stronger than before."

"Cut out that false camaraderie;
Prepare to meet your destiny."
"I don't quite understand," says Al.
"Are you perhaps joking with me?"
"You'll pay for your vile felony,"
Don Carlo says. "Soon you will see."
"Oh, now I see it clear," says Al.
"You broke your sacred vow, Grandee."

"So what," says Carlo, mad as hell,
"And that goes for that Jezebel;
My sister, who else would I mean;
She made the Calatrava name unclean."
"She lives," cries Al. "That lamb of God,
You tell me that she's living still?
I'll find and wed her on the spot."
Don Carlo says, "Like hell you will."

ACT IV, SCENE 1 *The Courtyard of the Church of the Angels Five Years Later*

Alvaro, now Fra Rafael,
Has donned the cloth, his soul to quell.
Leonore's practically next door,
'Mid rocks and crags in her dim cell.
Don Carlo, still on vengeance bound,
Has found the holy, pious place.
He swears this time Alvaro'll die;
He'll pay the price for his disgrace.

Within the holy citadel,
He asks to see Fra Rafael.
Alvaro greets Carlo with joy,
Much more that even tongue can tell.
"Just knock off all that camaraderie,
And all that phony 'glad to see.'
This time you'll die, or maybe me.
It all depends on destiny."

"Have mercy on a penitent."
Alvaro drops the sword upon the ground.
"Let not Hell triumph, go in peace,"
Then bows his head in prayer profound.
"You flout me, coward, mulatto base,"
Then slaps the friar in the face.
"You've sealed your fate," says Fra Rafael.
"Let it be death."—Away they race.

SCENE 2 – *A Valley amid Rocks; a Stream;*
also a Cave

Leonore takes a breath, then prays
For death and hopes it will come soon.
We hear the sound of clashing swords
As the belligerents near their doom.
Leonore rushes to her cave, with sobs and
    tears,
And moans and sighs.
She shuts the door, sad and heart-sore,
And then she starts to vocalize.

Again a dying voice is heard,
"Rush for a priest, my soul to save.
I must be shriven 'fore I die."
Alvaro rushes to the cave.
"Please, Mr. Hermit, please, I beg.
A man who's dying must confess."
"I cannot come, can't tell you why;
I'm not allowed to shrive or bless."

"A woman's voice. Ah, no, a ghost!
I'm going mad. It cannot be."
Santa Maria, it is Leonore.
He starts to swoon and says, "It's she."
Wounded and more dead than alive,
Supported by some dear old monks,
Before he dies, Carlo revives,
And stabs Leonore to death, the skunk.

"How odd of God," Alvaro sobs,
"To wreak this vengeance on Leonore."
"Please hold your tongue," a friar says.
"How dare you question El Señor?"
'Mid psalms and tears, praises and prayers,
"Gloria in Excelsis" everywhere.
Leonore dies, amid good-byes,
And vows to met her love Up There!

ACT I

The lover's a painter in love with a dame
Named Floria Tosca, a diva of fame.
He sings, as he paints, of strange harmonies,
But tenors are strange; I'm sure you'll agree.

The villian's a baron, a chief of police,
And he's hot for La Tosca, the great cantatrice.
His passion's for real; it's not a caprice.
And his project is worse than the rape of Lucrèce.

The runaway convict is l'Angelotti,
A political prisoner—a *corroboree.*
He escapes to a church and runs vis-à-vis
To the painter, the liberal, Cavaradossi.

They shake hands and vow with warm bonhomie.
He'll come to the aid of the party, says he!
A box lunch he hands him and tells him to flee.
"Quick, hide in the niche of the Attavanti!"

A voice is now heard. The timing's absurd.
It's Tosca, the diva, the jealous songbird.
She enters distraught, distracted, disturbed;
Calls Mario a two-timing, terrible word.

TOSCA

"I heard voices and fluttering skirts sneak away."
"Oh, come now," says Mario. "Please don't be that way.
I adore you. How could I my siren betray?"
They embrace and in parting we hear Tosca say,

"*Ciao,* my beloved, my sweet Sybarite.
Tonight in my villa, we'll make it a night.
We'll bill and we'll coo as two lovebirds might.
Come to the stage door to fetch me, all right?"

He then calls the jailbird, "Come out; it's okay.
My jealous enchantress is out of the way."
Then right at this moment they halt in dismay.
A cannon is fired. Cops are on their way.

"The manhunt is on. You must get away.
Go jump in the well," we hear Mario say.
"The well's in my garden. I'll show you the way."
Both hop, skip, and jump along the pathway.

Scarpia bursts in like a bat out of hell.
He'll slay, draw and quarter, the red infidel.
He knows where he's at; he's followed the smell.
In no time at all, he'll be back in his cell.

She's back on the scene; Miss Tosca, I mean;
Runs smash into Scarpia, the bigot supreme.
He drools at the mouth, mean and obscene.
What luck. A decoy. A go-in-between.

Scarpia tells her her lover did play;
Had a roll in the hay with a blonde yesterday.
Her rage knows no bounds; swears he'll rue the day;
Then runs from the church as the fuzz kneels to pray.

Act II

Scarpia's having a bite by dim candlelight
In his palace abode, feeling mean and contrite.
How could he foresee his plan for delight
Would be his last supper, his very last night?

By his *salle à manger* he has what one might say
A homey idea of an *auto de fè*.
His houseguest is Mario, arrested today.
He screams in B flats while they torture away.

She's back on the scene, Miss Tosca, his dream.
'Twas Scarpia's idea, the lecherous fiend.
He'll coax and he'll scream till she spills the beans
Then have for himself (you know what I mean).

The superb *Vissi d'art* she starts tearing apart.
Lying prone on the floor with tears and Del Sarte,
She wiggles and tries to melt his hard heart.
He couldn't care less; so one asks, "What is art?"

As the pig continues the cruel third degree,
There's a shrill scream of pain. It's C above B.
It's the voice of her lover, Cavaradossi.
She's had it, then sobs, "In the well," helplessly.

The torture is o'er. Then bleeding and sore
Her lover limps in, dripping over with gore.
She runs to his aid and confesses once more
That she spilled the beans to the inquisitor.

"Dear God, what you've done, my cherished loved one.
You've betrayed us and lost the battle hard won."
"Enough," cries the fuzz, the copper, the scum.
"To the gallows the painter. Let justice be done!"

"Now, Tosca," says he, "it's between you and me."
"What's the price for his life?" in a daze murmurs she.
"The price for his life is as simple can be.
It's you, my proud beauty; I hope you'll agree."

Distraught and distracted beyond all degree
She pleads with the pig to let Mario free.
"Upon that condition," he chortles with glee.
She knows she's defeated; she nods, meaning *sí*.

Delighted, the lecher, the mean debauchee,
Writes the safe conduct, the planned mockery.
He goes to the dame with the false assignee,
Breathes heavy, and sighs, "Now sock it to me!"

In the meantime our Tosca, distraught as can be,
Picked from the table a knife secretly.
So 'twas she and not he that stuck it in, see?
Take that, you old monster. You son of a B.

She looks down in dread to make sure that he's dead.
She then places two candles alight by his head,
Snatches the pass from his right hand outspread,
Then cautiously leaves in a slow-measured tread.

ACT III

Getting ready to die as the dawn breaks the sky,
Mario sings of his nearing demise.
Life never was sweeter, he moans, and he sighs
For voluptuous Tosca, the light of his eyes.

While shedding hot tears a voice now he hears.
It's Floria Tosca, her steps drawing near.
She falls in his arms, starts wiping his tears.
With love and caresses, she calms all his fears.

"Do banish your fears and sad thoughts, dearest pet."
Then she whispers, "I killed the vile martinet.
The thing that he asked for he sure didn't get,
But I got the pass, love, with blood, tears, and sweat.

"We're as free as the air," she sighs in his ear.
"Here is the pass. The coast is all clear.
Together we'll cross this lousy frontier.
Now listen to me, my brave musketeer.

"The shooting, my love, is only a sham."
Surprised, he says, "Really? Well, gee. I'll be damned."
"It's all in the bag, adored one, my lamb.
When they shoot you, drop, then later we'll scram."

The soldiers march in, take aim, and then stand.
They're given the signal; they fire at the man.
He falls to the ground; the action is grand.
They march away proudly, according to plan.

Fearful and breathless La Tosca appears.
"You've played your part well. Don't move yet, my dear.
They're now out of sight. The coast is all clear.
Get up, my beloved, arise. Don't you hear?

"My God," Tosca screams. "They've shot him for real.
The vile double-dealers, the villains, the heels."
She screams and she cries; she yells and she squeals.
Her oaths reach the skies; her own doom is sealed.

The murder is out. She's done it and goofed.
The thugs point to Tosca, defiant, aloof.
"No more will Cock Robin connive, threat, and spoof,"
She snarls at the henchmen, then jumps off the roof.

ACT I, SCENE I

When Rhadames met Aida 'twas love at first sight.
She too felt the same, as two lovers might.
They sneaked behind rocks and behind the palm trees
Where they couldn't be seen if they dropped their chemise.

He calls her celestial, a shapely sweetheart,
As he's planning to tear all her people apart;
He'll crown her with glory, just like a queen.
He'll give her his all, if you know what I mean.

He goes on to sing that he'll give·her the sky,
A throne in the sun, no expense is too high.
With so much emotion, desire, and all that,
No wonder most tenors crack on the B flat.

While all this deceit and deception goes on,
A messenger, jogging, runs through the throng.
He announces that Thebes' been invaded and, too,
That M. F. Amonasro is planning a coup.

"My dad," sighs Aida, stifling a sob.
"Why does he come now, with the rest of those slobs?"
She's torn between love and duty, poor thing.
She's just too upset, so she starts in to sing.

 IDA

ACT II – *Amneris' Apartment*

Princess Amneris is lovesick on the couch,
For that guileful, deceptive, two-timing slouch.
Her wise plans are laid (so're Aida's, the slave).
She'll fight to the finish; she rants and she raves.

Amneris' stress is cooled more or less
By the slaves that are fanning away her distress.
She then calls Aida to come to her side.
Aida's prepared for the worst, mystified.

"Now I must explain," says Amneris, aflame.
"The captain, courageous Rhadames, was slain."
Then green-eyed with scorn, she asks, "Can you mourn?"
"Forever I'll mourn," says Aida, forlorn.

"Fie," screams Amneris. "The cat's out of the bag."
"You love him, I know," she shrieks like a hag.
"But tremble, you slave, you dusky upstart.
With my very hands, I'll tear you apart!"

"Yes, you're my rival," defeated, she bleats.
Thus saying, Aida starts getting cold feet.
She falls to her knees, begs, and implores
For mercy and pity; she's worse than before.

A flurry of trumpets and festive fanfare
Is heard clear and loud; cries of joy fill the air.
Amneris prepares to attend on the throne.
Aida must come; she'll throw her a bone.

Thebes Again

The trombones and horns step right out of the pit,
Don diapers and helmets, and things that don't fit.
Amneris and King take their place on the throne.
Everyone is on stage; there's nobody home.

In the middle of this, in a litter of gold,
Under a canopy, lost in the folds,
Is the conqueror Rhadames, lying supine,
Done up like an idol en route to a shrine.

"Bring on the captives," Rhadames screams.
The basketball players rush in with their team.
Amonasro's among them, done up in a skin.
"Land sakes, that's my daddy," cries our heroine.

Her loud sotto voce is heard by them all.
"Her daddy!" they thunder, right through the hall.
Queries King, "Who are you?" to Amonasro.
"I'm Aida's dad, that's who I am, Bo.

"And look, Mr. King, you know well as I do
What happened to me could have happened to you.
So I beg of Your Majesty, set my men free."
"Ye gods," cries out Ramfis. "How nuts can he be?"

King finally says, "Oh, let them all go.
One's quite enough; keep Amonasro.
He can stay with his daughter, Aida; that's fine.
We'll know where to find him should he get out of line."

The high priest turns pale, starts chewing his nails.
"You'll be sorry," he says as he moans and he wails.
"They did it before and they'll do it some more."
"So what," says King, as he starts to get sore.

He descends from the throne, says, "Please leave me alone,"
And to Rhadames says, "There's no place like home.
You fought for your land, so I give you the hand,
Of my daughter, Amneris, to rule o'er this land."

The last thing he wants is King's daughter's hand,
But he's now in a bind—a command's a command.
To escape from the wiles of this dame of the Nile
Will take some conniving, scheming, and guile.

ACT III – *The Nile Scene*

The Nile flows along as the Nile always does,
Murky and dull and impervious.
Meanwhile Aida sneaks on the scene
With a veil on her head, thinking she won't be seen.

Although it's quite late, she's keeping a date
To meet Rhadames and talk over their fate.
She trembles with fear that he'll give her the air
Or tell her what was, and end it all there.

As she plans her demise, she gets a surprise.
"Great heaven," she cries, as her father she spies.
She expected her beau, but it's that big bozo
Amonasro, her dad, the old so and so.

"I know you're in love with that whitey," he said.
"But listen here, honey, you're being misled.
I don't trust that race; they're meaner than apes;
And your brethren and sistern are all getting raped."

Aida is shocked. She covers her face,
But the scenes of her homeland she cannot efface.
The forest primeval Aida recalls,
The temples, the vales, she was princess of all.

Her father insists that for her own country's sake
She find out the path the Egyptians will take.
In terror and woe, she answers, "No, no."
"Have pity." She begs, so he cracks her a blow.

"Have courage; he comes," he tells her and runs.
He hides behind palm trees as Rhadames comes.
Radiant with joy, the lover appears.
"Aida," he sighs. "How nice you are here."

"Don't Aida me, you phony," says she.
"You belong to Amneris," she repeats scornfully.
"I love you, Aida. Please don't get that way;
And, dear, I've an alibi. Listen, I pray."

"If you really love me, we both can be free
In dear old Ethiopia, just you and me."
"I?" he replied. "Leave my country?" He sighed.
"Live among strangers, those black, evil guys?"

"Okay, this is it, so let's call it quits."
She's got Rhadames by the perquisites.
Love must find a way. He's got to obey.
For a roll in the hay, his land he'll betray.

"What road do we take," she asks, "by the way?"
"By the gorges of Napata; let's leave right away."
"Atta boy—Napata," we hear a voice say.
If it ain't Old Man River screaming hurray.

"Dishonored, a traitor! Aida, for you.
Betrayer of country; ye gods, I am through."
Chagrined and distracted, embarrassed with shame,
"You done it," he says. "Only you are to blame."

"Traitor. Betrayer," we hear a voice scream.
It's the voice of Amneris, venting her spleen.
He's caught in the act, with his pants down—and how!
Now for sure he will land in the Memphis hoosegow.

"Run. Get away," we hear Rhadames say
To Aida and dad, who start fleeing away.
Amonasro, en route, stops only to try
To slay Amneris, but his try goes awry.

ACT IV – *A Hall in the Palace*

In the hall of the palace, Amneris's alone,
Mad 'cause Aida, the blackbird, has flown.
She accuses the lovers of sly double takes,
But because she loves Rhad, she'll plead for his sake.

She summons the guards to bring Rhadames.
She comforts and says, "You're sure in a mess.
If you'll listen to me, I can still be of help.
I don't have to tell you, the priests want your scalp.

Of course, Rhadames, you must promise you'll part
From your ebony girlfriend—that two-timing tart.
You and I can be happy, this I guarantee.
You'll get out of this pickle; leave it to me."

"Why should I explain to those mummies?" he said.
"And without Aida, I'd rather be dead.
You were jealous, Amneris, right from the start;
So you had her slain, just to keep us apart."

"Okay, Rhadames. Since you turn me down flat,
Though I offered to give you my all and all that,
Aida, the snip, gave the gendarmes the slip,
And that ass Amonasro was slain—the old drip."

"So you waited till now to tell me, you witch,
Hoping I'd give my loved one the ditch.
So I'd rather, much rather, be smothered and die;
So get the message, Amneris—Good-bye."

Scorned and disdained, she lingers awhile.
For not taking no for an answer, herself she reviles.
"I did it," she says as the priest crosses the stage.
"I alone am to blame," she cries in a rage.

The high priests and Ramfis decide Rhad must die.
"Wretches, assassins," Amneris screams high.
But those Egyptian malfactors, corrupt, are hell-bent
To bury the guy in a coat of cement.

ACT V – *Room in the Palace Hall and Prison Cell*

"Aida," Rhad moans in the tomb all alone,
As the stone slowly drops in his dread catacomb.
He feels being groped. No doubt it's a joke.
"In very poor taste of Isis," he mopes.

Then all of a sudden he screams in high C,
"Ye gods, it's Aida" (there on the QT).
"Don't think it was easy to slip in," she sighs.
"'Twas a sure tour de force to slip by those guys."

She falls in his arms. They both start to sing.
"How nice it's to die. Death, where is thy sting?"
As the stone downward slides, the skies open wide.
Two more go to heaven to live side by side.